Daily Editing

◉ Grade 5 ◉

by Linda Armstrong

Carson-Dellosa Publishing Company, Inc.
Greensboro, North Carolina

Dedication

For my husband, Alden, with thanks for his patience, and for Jennifer, with appreciation for her patience and support.

Credits

Editor: Carrie Fox

Layout Design: Lori Jackson

Cover Design: Lori Jackson

Cover Photo: © 2007 JupiterImages Corporation

This book has been correlated to state, national, and Canadian provincial standards. Visit *www.carsondellosa.com* to search for and view its correlations to your standards.

Table of Contents

Table of Contents

Grammar and Usage

Spelling

Complete Sentences

Putting It All Together

Appendix

Daily Editing

Introduction

Daily Editing provides teachers with an effective structure for reinforcing and assessing students' editing and proofreading skills using standard writing conventions. Students need daily practice with capitalization, punctuation, grammar, spelling, and sentence structure to ensure proficiency. This book fosters the development of these conventions and editing skills through frequent, focused practice.

Daily Editing includes 180 grade-appropriate fiction and nonfiction passages (including journal entries, e-mails, and letters) that provide material for students' practice. Each basic practice page focuses on one or more proofreading marks within the context of appropriate conventions. Reviews provide additional practice of the introduced skills in a sequential, cumulative manner.

This resource contains:

- A detailed table of contents to help teachers identify targeted writing conventions
- Student pages with error overviews to guide students in editing
- Answer key pages with all errors corrected using appropriate proofreading marks
- A Proofreader's Marks Chart to teach and reinforce standard proofreading marks
- An Editing Checklist that highlights basic rules for writing and editing
- A Grammar Glossary for students and teachers to use as a reference

How to Use This Book

Daily Editing can be used in a variety of ways depending on instructional goals and students' needs. Determine the approach that is most effective for your students.

1. Use each passage as a directed lesson for the whole class.

Conduct a mini-lesson on a targeted convention and the appropriate proofreading mark. Then, display an overhead transparency of the chosen passage. Read the passage aloud and note the number of errors cited on the answer key page. Reread the passage, pausing between the sentences. Correct the errors as a class using the appropriate marks.

2. Use each passage as an independent lesson for small groups or pairs of students.

Before beginning, familiarize students with a targeted convention and the appropriate proofreading mark. Then, give each group or pair a copy of the chosen passage. Direct students in each group or pair to work together to identify the errors and correct them using the appropriate proofreading mark. When each group or pair is finished, display an overhead transparency of the passage and identify the errors as a class. (If desired, invite students to identify each error and to determine the associated convention.)

3. Use each passage as independent practice for individual students.

Give each student a copy of the chosen passage. Direct students to read the passage, identify the errors, and use the appropriate proofreading marks to correct them. When students are finished, display an overhead transparency of the passage and identify the errors as a class.

A Special Afternoon

November 6, 2011

Dear Journal,

Today, my Mom and Dad took me to meet governor Marcus Christopher. The Governor was speaking at our convention center. We met aunt Rose and uncle Derek in the lobby. My aunt and Uncle followed mom and me to our seats. My father said that he would meet us later. He waved to reverend Dawson, who was standing at a side door. Then, he hurried off to join him. I was so proud when I saw dad on the stage. He introduced the Reverend first. Then, he introduced mayor Benitez. The Mayor introduced the Governor. After the program, dad personally introduced us to all of them. It was a very special afternoon.

ERRORS: MAKE UPPERCASE: 8; MAKE LOWERCASE: 8

The Graduation Ceremony

Last June, my whole family attended my older Brother's graduation. It was almost like a family reunion. When my Grandmother arrived from Toronto, mom and I picked her up at the airport. Uncle Taron and aunt Ruth came in their car. They brought Jeff, my Cousin. The night before the ceremony, dad drove to Williamston to pick up grandpa. The event was held on the football field. The guest speakers included coach Warren, mayor Chesterfield, governor Kirkpatrick, and rabbi T. S. Monroe. My little Sister fell asleep in the middle of dean Shelby's introduction. My favorite part of the ceremony was when principal Ryan congratulated the class and the graduates tossed their caps into the air. That night, my Mother drove us to a Chinese restaurant in a rented van. My Uncle gave my Brother a watch that had once belonged to our Great-Grandfather.

ERRORS: MAKE UPPERCASE: 10; MAKE LOWERCASE: 9

Name: _____ Date: _____

A Special Afternoon ①

November 6, 2011

Dear Journal,

Today, my Mom and Dad took me to meet governor Marcus Christopher. The Governor was speaking at our convention center. We met aunt Rose and uncle Derek in the lobby. My aunt and Uncle followed mom and me to our seats. My Father said that he would meet us later. He waved to reverend Dawson, who was standing at a side door. Then, he hurried off to join him. I was so proud when I saw dad on the stage. He introduced the Reverend first. Then, he introduced mayor Benitez. The Mayor introduced the Governor. After the program, dad personally introduced us to all of them. It was a very special afternoon.

✔ LOOK FOR: FAMILY NAMES AND OFFICIAL TITLES

Name: _____ Date: _____

The Graduation Ceremony ②

Last June, my whole family attended my older Brother's graduation. It was almost like a family reunion. When my Grandmother arrived from Toronto, mom and I picked her up at the airport. Uncle Taron and aunt Ruth came in their car. They brought Jeff, my Cousin. The night before the ceremony, dad drove to Williamston to pick up grandpa. The event was held on the football field. The guest speakers included coach Warren, mayor Chesterfield, governor Kirkpatrick, and rabbi T. S. Monroe. My little Sister fell asleep in the middle of dean Shelby's introduction. My favorite part of the ceremony was when principal Ryan congratulated the class and the graduates tossed their caps into the air. That night, my Mother drove us to a Chinese restaurant in a rented van. My Uncle gave my Brother a watch that had once belonged to our Great-Grandfather.

✔ LOOK FOR: FAMILY NAMES AND OFFICIAL TITLES

Languages of the World

The people of the world speak many languages. The most commonly spoken languages are english and mandarin. Many australians, New Zealanders, South africans, canadians, and citizens of the United States speak English. Many Chinese people speak mandarin. Two languages from India, hindi and urdu, are spoken by about one-sixth of Earth's population. Other widely spoken languages include spanish, russian, bengali, malay, portuguese, japanese, french, and german.

ERRORS: MAKE UPPERCASE: 16

Religious Groups in Canada

People of many faiths live in Canada. Many early settlers were french roman catholics. Today, the largest religious group in Canada is still catholic. Many canadians are protestants. The largest protestant churches in the country are the united church of Canada and the anglican church of Canada. Jews, muslims, buddhists, hindus, and sikhs also make their homes in the nation.

ERRORS: MAKE UPPERCASE: 15

Name: _____ Date: _____

Languages of the World ③

The people of the world speak many languages. The most commonly spoken languages are english and mandarin. Many australians, New Zealanders, South africans, canadians, and citizens of the United States speak English. Many Chinese people speak mandarin. Two languages from India, hindi and urdu, are spoken by about one-sixth of Earth's population. Other widely spoken languages include spanish, russian, bengali, malay, portuguese, japanese, french, and german.

✔ LOOK FOR: NATIONALITIES, LANGUAGES, AND RELIGIONS

Name: _____ Date: _____

Religious Groups in Canada ④

People of many faiths live in Canada. Many early settlers were french roman catholics. Today, the largest religious group in Canada is still catholic. Many canadians are protestants. The largest protestant churches in the country are the united church of Canada and the anglican church of Canada. Jews, muslims, buddhists, hindus, and sikhs also make their homes in the nation.

✔ LOOK FOR: NATIONALITIES, LANGUAGES, AND RELIGIONS

5 | Works of Art at the Louvre

If you visit the Louvre, one of the world's greatest art museums, you will find paintings from many countries. You will see works by the italian artist Leonardo da Vinci, the dutch artist Rembrandt, the french artist Pierre Auguste Renoir, the belgian artist Rogier van der Weyden, the spanish artist El Greco, the german artist Hans Holbein, and the english artist Sir Joshua Reynolds. Great works from the ancient world, including the famous greek sculpture, The Winged Victory of Samothrace, are also displayed in the museum.

ERRORS: MAKE UPPERCASE: 7

6 | Food from Around the World

My mom took me to lunch downtown last Saturday. She wanted to eat someplace different. We parked near a russian restaurant. I wanted to try that, but Mom said that we should keep looking. On the next block, there was a belgian chocolate shop and an art gallery filled with italian marble sculptures. Next to the gallery was a french sidewalk cafe. I wanted to try it, but Mom wanted to keep looking. We walked past a german restaurant, a polish restaurant, a japanese tea garden, a thai restaurant, a tibetan restaurant, a mongolian stir fry place, a korean noodle house, an australian steak house, a danish bakery, and a spanish seafood house. Finally, we came to the mandarin chinese restaurant where we always eat. Mom held the door for me, and I walked in. "It would be nice to try someplace different one day," I said.

ERRORS: MAKE UPPERCASE: 16

Name: _____ Date: _____

Works of Art at the Louvre (5)

If you visit the Louvre, one of the world's greatest art museums, you will find paintings from many countries. You will see works by the italian artist Leonardo da Vinci, the dutch artist Rembrandt, the french artist Pierre Auguste Renoir, the belgian artist Rogier van der Weyden, the spanish artist El Greco, the german artist Hans Holbein, and the english artist Sir Joshua Reynolds. Great works from the ancient world, including the famous greek sculpture, The Winged Victory of Samothrace, are also displayed in the museum.

✔ LOOK FOR: NATIONALITIES

Name: _____ Date: _____

Food from Around the World (6)

My mom took me to lunch downtown last Saturday. She wanted to eat someplace different. We parked near a russian restaurant. I wanted to try that, but Mom said that we should keep looking. On the next block, there was a belgian chocolate shop and an art gallery filled with italian marble sculptures. Next to the gallery was a french sidewalk cafe. I wanted to try it, but Mom wanted to keep looking. We walked past a german restaurant, a polish restaurant, a japanese tea garden, a thai restaurant, a tibetan restaurant, a mongolian stir fry place, a korean noodle house, an australian steak house, a danish bakery, and a spanish seafood house. Finally, we came to the mandarin chinese restaurant where we always eat. Mom held the door for me, and I walked in. "It would be nice to try someplace different one day," I said.

✔ LOOK FOR: NATIONALITIES

Solar System Science Report

May 5, 2010

Dear Journal,

I have almost finished my science report. I have written about mercury, venus, earth, and mars. They are called the terrestrial planets. Now, I am working on the gaseous planets. My favorite planet is saturn, but jupiter, uranus, and neptune are interesting too. I will write a special paragraph about the dwarf planet, pluto, and the other objects at the edge of our solar system. If I finish my report before this weekend, Dad will take me to see the sharks play the barracudas at the Kennedy Downtown Arena. Last year, the sharks were almost the northeast champions. The orcas defeated them in the finals. The game is on Saturday afternoon.

 ERRORS: MAKE UPPERCASE: 14

Canada's Geographic Regions

Canada has eight geographic regions. The pacific ranges and lowlands include islands, mountains, valleys, and plains on or near the Pacific coast. The Rocky Mountains are part of a huge range that stretches down through the United States. The Arctic Islands lie in the frigid arctic. The interior plains, once a sea of grass, are now productive farms and ranches. The canadian shield, the country's largest region, is rich in mineral resources. The hudson bay lowlands are swampy. The St. lawrence lowlands are densely populated. In fact, more than half of Canada's people live there. The appalachian region is an area of hills, woods, and bays along the Atlantic coast.

ERRORS: MAKE UPPERCASE: 15

Name: _____   Date: _____

Solar System Science Report (7)

May 5, 2010

Dear Journal,

I have almost finished my science report. I have written about mercury, venus, earth, and mars. They are called the terrestrial planets. Now, I am working on the gaseous planets. My favorite planet is saturn, but jupiter, uranus, and neptune are interesting too. I will write a special paragraph about the dwarf planet, pluto, and the other objects at the edge of our solar system. If I finish my report before this weekend, Dad will take me to see the sharks play the barracudas at the Kennedy Downtown Arena. Last year, the sharks were almost the northeast champions. The orcas defeated them in the finals. The game is on Saturday afternoon.

✔ LOOK FOR: NAMES OF REGIONS, PLANETS, AND SPORTS TEAMS

Name: _____   Date: _____

Canada's Geographic Regions (8)

Canada has eight geographic regions. The pacific ranges and lowlands include islands, mountains, valleys, and plains on or near the Pacific coast. The Rocky Mountains are part of a huge range that stretches down through the United States. The Arctic Islands lie in the frigid arctic. The interior plains, once a sea of grass, are now productive farms and ranches. The canadian shield, the country's largest region, is rich in mineral resources. The hudson bay lowlands are swampy. The St. lawrence lowlands are densely populated. In fact, more than half of Canada's people live there. The appalachian region is an area of hills, woods, and bays along the Atlantic coast.

✔ LOOK FOR: NAMES OF REGIONS

CAPITALIZATION

 Geology through the Ages

Geologists have divided Earth's history into eras. The most recent is the cenozoic era. The Cenozoic is divided into the following periods: the tertiary and the quaternary. The tertiary period began at the end of the mesozoic era, which is sometimes known as the age of the dinosaurs. The tertiary is divided into the following epochs: the paleocene, the eocene, the oligocene, the miocene, and the pliocene. The quaternary, the most recent period, is divided into two epochs, the pleistocene and the holocene. Scientists have learned about geologic eras by studying rock layers and fossils.

ERRORS: MAKE UPPERCASE: 19

 Time Travel Costume Party

My friends and I are planning a time travel party. Everyone will dress in a costume that represents a different period in history. Zoe's mother is making an outfit for her. It will be similar to dresses that women wore during the renaissance. Rudy is wearing a peasant's costume from the middle ages. Travis has chosen a toga from the roman empire. Quincy is wearing an outfit from the persian empire. Steven is dressing as a sailor from the age of exploration, and Nina is wearing a mill worker's outfit from the industrial revolution. Because he loves the space age, Pablo is wearing an astronaut costume. Wendy is dressing as a girl from the age of pioneers, and Penny is dressing as a woman from the great depression. My brother and I are building a time machine gate for our door. It is just a box with a tape recorder and some lights, but we are sure that everyone will love it.

ERRORS: MAKE UPPERCASE: 17

Name: _____ Date: _____

Geology through the Ages 〈9〉

Geologists have divided Earth's history into eras. The most recent is the cenozoic era. The Cenozoic is divided into the following periods: the tertiary and the quaternary. The tertiary period began at the end of the mesozoic era, which is sometimes known as the age of the dinosaurs. The tertiary is divided into the following epochs: the paleocene, the eocene, the oligocene, the miocene, and the pliocene. The quaternary, the most recent period, is divided into two epochs, the pleistocene and the holocene. Scientists have learned about geologic eras by studying rock layers and fossils.

✔ LOOK FOR: GEOLOGIC ERAS, PERIODS, AND EPOCHS

Name: _____ Date: _____

Time Travel Costume Party 〈10〉

My friends and I are planning a time travel party. Everyone will dress in a costume that represents a different period in history. Zoe's mother is making an outfit for her. It will be similar to dresses that women wore during the renaissance. Rudy is wearing a peasant's costume from the middle ages. Travis has chosen a toga from the roman empire. Quincy is wearing an outfit from the persian empire. Steven is dressing as a sailor from the age of exploration, and Nina is wearing a mill worker's outfit from the industrial revolution. Because he loves the space age, Pablo is wearing an astronaut costume. Wendy is dressing as a girl from the age of pioneers, and Penny is dressing as a woman from the great depression. My brother and I are building a time machine gate for our door. It is just a box with a tape recorder and some lights, but we are sure that everyone will love it.

✔ LOOK FOR: HISTORICAL PERIODS

11 | Pamela's Heritage

Pamela's mother is very proud that her relatives are italian catholics. They came to this country from Italy during the industrial revolution. Her family worked hard and built a business. They lost their money in the great depression, but they did not give up. Pamela's grandfather is a retired Professor, and her mother is a doctor. Last week, governor Taylor and mayor Spenser came to participate in the city's annual Immigrant's Day Parade. There were english, french, Russian, german, and scandanavian floats. Pamela and her Mother rode on the italian float with father Thomas, a Priest from their church. Some popular players from the spartans, our local hockey team, were there too. The float depicted the mathematician and pioneer astronomer Galileo gazing at mars through a telescope.

ERRORS: MAKE UPPERCASE: 16; MAKE LOWERCASE: 3

12 | The Warriors Basketball Team

On Saturday, dad took my brother and me to a special event at Municipal Auditorium downtown. It was a tribute to the warriors, our city's basketball team. Every player stood up and told about himself and his family. I learned that several of the players are bilingual. Two of the players speak french, two speak spanish, and one speaks german. All of these languages are useful when the team travels to Europe during the off-season. The players come from many different religious backgrounds. Some are muslim, others are catholic, one is jewish, one is lutheran, and another is buddhist. When games are played on religious holidays, team members cover for each other. The combination has been successful so far. Last season, the warriors were the champions of the pacific northwest.

ERRORS: MAKE UPPERCASE: 13; MAKE LOWERCASE: 1

Name: _____ Date: _____

Pamela's Heritage (11)

Pamela's mother is very proud that her relatives are italian catholics. They came

to this country from Italy during the industrial revolution. Her family worked hard

and built a business. They lost their money in the great depression, but they did

not give up. Pamela's grandfather is a retired Professor, and her mother is a doctor.

Last week, governor Taylor and mayor Spenser came to participate in the city's

annual Immigrant's Day Parade. There were english, french, Russian, german, and

scandanavian floats. Pamela and her Mother rode on the italian float with father

Thomas, a Priest from their church. Some popular players from the spartans, our local

hockey team, were there too. The float depicted the mathematician and pioneer

astronomer Galileo gazing at mars through a telescope.

✔ MIXED REVIEW

Name: _____ Date: _____

The Warriors Basketball Team (12)

On Saturday, dad took my Brother and me to a special event at Municipal Auditorium

downtown. It was a tribute to the warriors, our city's basketball team. Every player

stood up and told about himself and his family. I learned that several of the players

are bilingual. Two of the players speak french, two speak spanish, and one speaks

german. All of these languages are useful when the team travels to Europe during

the off-season. The players come from many different religious backgrounds. Some

are muslim, others are catholic, one is jewish, one is lutheran, and another is buddhist.

When games are played on religious holidays, team members cover for each other.

The combination has been successful so far. Last season, the warriors were the

champions of the pacific northwest.

✔ MIXED REVIEW

13 A Dramatic Invitation

To: audrey@nomail.zap
From: betsy@nomail.zap

Dear Audrey,

On Saturday, Mom is taking me to see a play at the bloomsbury playhouse. Would you like to join us there at 2:00 P.M.? The playhouse is at 212 w. spring street next to the regents hotel. It is about two blocks from banks park. After the play, we will eat at the carter café on brady drive. You will love it! I am sorry we cannot pick you up, but Mom has a dental appointment in the addison medical building on First street at 12:30 P.M. The building is close to the playhouse, but your house is a little too far away. I hope you can come!

Your friend,
Betsy

✗ ERRORS: MAKE UPPERCASE: 17

----

14 A Day about Town

To: anthony@nomail.zap
From: eugene@nomail.zap

Dear Tony,

James and I are planning to go to the glen hills Central library next weekend to find some books and pictures for our report. Would you like to meet us there? The library is downtown on north Lilac boulevard between kenyon's music store and green plains county courthouse. My dad will pick us up at lunchtime. He is planning to take us to the glen Hills butterfly house and botanical gardens on lost Creek Road. There are some great trails in the hills above the greenhouse. I hope you can join us. Please call me soon.

Your friend,
Gene

✗ ERRORS: MAKE UPPERCASE: 18

Name: _____ Date: _____

A Dramatic Invitation (13)

To: audrey@nomail.zap
From: betsy@nomail.zap

Dear Audrey,

On Saturday, Mom is taking me to see a play at the bloomsbury playhouse. Would you like to join us there at 2:00 P.M.? The playhouse is at 212 w. spring street next to the regents hotel. It is about two blocks from banks park. After the play, we will eat at the carter café on brady drive. You will love it! I am sorry we cannot pick you up, but Mom has a dental appointment in the addison medical building on First street at 12:30 P.M. The building is close to the playhouse, but your house is a little too far away. I hope you can come!

Your friend,
Betsy

✔ LOOK FOR: STREETS AND SPECIFIC PLACES IN THE UNITED STATES

Name: _____ Date: _____

A Day about Town (14)

To: anthony@nomail.zap
From: eugene@nomail.zap

Dear Tony,

James and I are planning to go to the glen hills Central library next weekend to find some books and pictures for our report. Would you like to meet us there? The library is downtown on north Lilac boulevard between kenyon's music store and green plains county courthouse. My dad will pick us up at lunchtime. He is planning to take us to the glen Hills butterfly house and botanical gardens on lost Creek Road. There are some great trails in the hills above the greenhouse. I hope you can join us. Please call me soon.

Your friend,
Gene

✔ LOOK FOR: STREETS AND SPECIFIC PLACES IN THE UNITED STATES

15 National Parks of the American West

Many spectacular national parks are located in the western United States. Travelers from around the world come to admire these natural wonders. Park visitors often visit nearby cities and towns. Arches National Park is close to the quaint city of moab, utah. Rainier National Park is close to cosmopolitan seattle, washington. Grand Canyon National Park is a train ride away from historic williams, arizona. Just a short drive from exciting denver, colorado is Rocky Mountain National Park. Zion National Park is less than an hour away from st. george, utah. Though its name is not impressive, scenic jackson hole, wyoming sits on the edge of Grand Teton National Park. The tourist town is also close to Yellowstone National Park. Crater Lake National Park, the site of a lake that formed after a volcanic explosion, is close to medford, oregon.

✗ ERRORS: MAKE UPPERCASE: 16

16 Musical Cities

Some U.S. cities are known for the kinds of music they produce. For example, new orleans, louisiana was the birthplace of Dixieland jazz. Another southern city, nashville, tennessee, is a center for country music. The city of detroit, michigan, is famous for the Motown record label that popularized soul music, as well as rhythm and blues. The Midwestern city of chicago, illinois is also known for its role in the development of jazz. The International Bluegrass Music Awards are held in louisville, kentucky. Los angeles, california, home of the Legendary Hollywood Boulevard, is a recording and distribution center for many kinds of music, including pop and film scores. New york, new york has also produced many styles of music, including musical comedies.

✗ ERRORS: MAKE UPPERCASE: 16

Name: _____ Date: _____

National Parks of the American West 15

Many spectacular national parks are located in the western United States. Travelers from around the world come to admire these natural wonders. Park visitors often visit nearby cities and towns. Arches National Park is close to the quaint city of moab, utah. Rainier National Park is close to cosmopolitan seattle, washington. Grand Canyon National Park is a train ride away from historic williams, arizona. Just a short drive from exciting denver, colorado is Rocky Mountain National Park. Zion National Park is less than an hour away from st. george, utah. Though its name is not impressive, scenic jackson hole, wyoming sits on the edge of Grand Teton National Park. The tourist town is also close to Yellowstone National Park. Crater Lake National Park, the site of a lake that formed after a volcanic explosion, is close to medford, oregon.

✔ LOOK FOR: U.S. CITIES AND STATES

Name: _____ Date: _____

Musical Cities 16

Some U.S. cities are known for the kinds of music they produce. For example, new orleans, louisiana was the birthplace of Dixieland jazz. Another southern city, nashville, tennessee, is a center for country music. The city of detroit, michigan, is famous for the Motown record label that popularized soul music, as well as rhythm and blues. The Midwestern city of chicago, illinois is also known for its role in the development of jazz. The International Bluegrass Music Awards are held in louisville, kentucky. Los angeles, california, home of the Legendary Hollywood Boulevard, is a recording and distribution center for many kinds of music, including pop and film scores. New york, new york has also produced many styles of music, including musical comedies.

✔ LOOK FOR: U.S. CITIES AND STATES

17 **Toronto Parks**

Toronto has many recreational areas. One of the largest is high park. Located just north of lake ontario, the park is bounded by several main streets. Bloor street west is on the north edge. On the east lies parkside drive. Ellis park road runs along the west edge, and lake shore boulevard west forms part of the southern boundary. This huge park contains beautiful gardens, playgrounds, a swimming pool, grassy fields, woods, and even a small zoo. Grenadier pond is popular all year. Fishermen love fishing there in the summer, and kids gather around it in the winter to build snowmen. Some people bring binoculars to gaze at the wild birds and other creatures that live along its marshy shores.

 ERRORS: MAKE UPPERCASE: 15

18 **Tourist Attractions in Victoria**

Victoria, British Columbia is considered one of the most beautiful cities in the world. About two million people flock to such attractions as the empress Hotel, thunderbird park, and butchart Gardens each year. Victoria is the capital of the province, and the impressive buildings of the british Columbia parliament are located there. Known for its mild climate, the city offers its citizens many recreational opportunities. For example, the victoria youth park at 250 esquimalt road is a skating facility. Everything in the park, including the basketball court, is skate accessible. The royal athletic park at 1014 caledonia avenue is a playing field with permanent seats and bleachers. As many as 9,000 people can watch soccer, Canadian football, baseball, or rugby there.

 ERRORS: MAKE UPPERCASE: 16

Name: _____ Date: _____

Toronto Parks (17)

Toronto has many recreational areas. One of the largest is high park. Located just

north of lake ontario, the park is bounded by several main streets. Bloor street west

is on the north edge. On the east lies parkside drive. Ellis park road runs along the

west edge, and lake shore boulevard west forms part of the southern boundary. This

huge park contains beautiful gardens, playgrounds, a swimming pool, grassy fields,

woods, and even a small zoo. Grenadier pond is popular all year. Fishermen love

fishing there in the summer, and kids gather around it in the winter to build snowmen.

Some people bring binoculars to gaze at the wild birds and other creatures that live

along its marshy shores.

✔ LOOK FOR: STREETS AND SPECIFIC PLACES IN CANADA

Name: _____ Date: _____

Tourist Attractions in Victoria (18)

Victoria, British Columbia is considered one of the most beautiful cities in the world.

About two million people flock to such attractions as the empress Hotel, thunderbird

park, and butchart Gardens each year. Victoria is the capital of the province, and the

impressive buildings of the british Columbia parliament are located there. Known for its

mild climate, the city offers its citizens many recreational opportunities. For example,

the victoria youth park at 250 esquimalt road is a skating facility. Everything in the park,

including the basketball court, is skate accessible. The royal athletic park at

1014 caledonia avenue is a playing field with permanent seats and bleachers. As

many as 9,000 people can watch soccer, Canadian football, baseball, or rugby there.

✔ LOOK FOR: STREETS AND SPECIFIC PLACES IN CANADA

Canadian Capitals

The people in each of Canada's provinces are proud of their capital cities. Built on a spot discovered by Europeans in 1497, St. john's is the capital of newfoundland and labrador. An important port city, halifax, is the capital of nova scotia. Established in 1785, fredericton is the capital of new brunswick. Named after Queen Charlotte, wife of King George III, charlottetown is the capital of prince edward island. The capital of the province of quebec is the elegant city of quebec, and the capital of ontario is cosmopolitan toronto. Bustling winnipeg, manitoba and beautiful Victoria, British Columbia are both provincial capitals.

 ERRORS: MAKE UPPERCASE: 19

Canada's Largest Metropolitan Areas and Cities

A metropolitan area includes a central city and its surrounding towns or suburbs. Canada's largest metropolitan area is toronto, ontario, and montreal, quebec is next in size. The third-largest metropolitan area is vancouver, british columbia, followed by ottawa-hull. Rounding out the top five metropolitan areas is edmonton, alberta. A list of the nation's largest cities is not the same because not all cities have a network of suburbs. If only actual city limits are considered, montreal is Canada's largest city. The second-largest city is calgary, alberta. Toronto is the third-largest city. Edmonton is still fifth on the list, but winnipeg, manitoba is fourth.

ERRORS: MAKE UPPERCASE: 16

Name: _____ Date: _____

Canadian Capitals (19)

The people in each of Canada's provinces are proud of their capital cities. Built on a
spot discovered by Europeans in 1497, St. john's is the capital of newfoundland and
labrador. An important port city, halifax, is the capital of nova scotia. Established in
1785, fredericton is the capital of new brunswick. Named after Queen Charlotte, wife
of King George III, charlottetown is the capital of prince edward island. The capital
of the province of quebec is the elegant city of quebec, and the capital of ontario
is cosmopolitan toronto. Bustling winnipeg, manitoba and beautiful Victoria, British
Columbia are both provincial capitals.

✔ LOOK FOR: CANADIAN CITIES AND PROVINCES

Name: _____ Date: _____

Canada's Largest Metropolitan Areas and Cities (20)

A metropolitan area includes a central city and its surrounding towns or suburbs.
Canada's largest metropolitan area is toronto, ontario, and montreal, quebec is next
in size. The third-largest metropolitan area is vancouver, british columbia, followed by
ottawa-hull. Rounding out the top five metropolitan areas is edmonton, alberta. A list
of the nation's largest cities is not the same because not all cities have a network of
suburbs. If only actual city limits are considered, montreal is Canada's largest city. The
second-largest city is calgary, alberta. Toronto is the third-largest city. Edmonton is still
fifth on the list, but winnipeg, manitoba is fourth.

✔ LOOK FOR: CANADIAN CITIES AND PROVINCES

21 Having Fun in Denver

Home to thousands of outdoor enthusiasts, denver, colorado is proud of its network of parks, trails, and recreational facilities. The largest of these facilities is city park on colorado boulevard. Designed in 1882, this popular park contains a zoo and a museum. Some denver parks, such as alamo placita park on speer boulevard, feature elegant formal gardens. Others, such as berkeley lake park on tennyson street, include recreation centers. Frequent visits to these beautiful islands of water, grass, and forest are an important part of life in the "Mile-High City."

ERRORS: MAKE UPPERCASE: 17

22 Historic Halifax

Established in 1749, halifax, nova scotia was the first permanent British settlement in Canada. The city has many historic structures. Since its opening on February 19, 1819, province house has served as the meeting place for the Nova Scotia State Legislature. It occupies an entire downtown block. On one side of the building is hollis street. Granville street, george street, and prince street also border the building. The halifax Citadel national Historic site is a major tourist attraction in the downtown area. The entrance to this fascinating fort complex is near the intersection of sackville street and Brunswick street.

ERRORS: MAKE UPPERCASE: 18

Name: _____ Date: _____

Having Fun in Denver **21**

Home to thousands of outdoor enthusiasts, denver, colorado is proud of its network of parks, trails, and recreational facilities. The largest of these facilities is city park on colorado boulevard. Designed in 1882, this popular park contains a zoo and a museum. Some denver parks, such as alamo placita park on speer boulevard, feature elegant formal gardens. Others, such as berkeley lake park on tennyson street, include recreation centers. Frequent visits to these beautiful islands of water, grass, and forest are an important part of life in the "Mile-High City."

✔ MIXED REVIEW

Name: _____ Date: _____

Historic Halifax **22**

Established in 1749, halifax, nova scotia was the first permanent British settlement in Canada. The city has many historic structures. Since its opening on February 19, 1819, province house has served as the meeting place for the Nova Scotia State Legislature. It occupies an entire downtown block. On one side of the building is hollis street. Granville street, george street, and prince street also border the building. The halifax Citadel national Historic site is a major tourist attraction in the downtown area. The entrance to this fascinating fort complex is near the intersection of sackville street and Brunswick street.

✔ MIXED REVIEW

24 Trading Card Mix-Up

154 s. Garrett ct.

pleasanton, Id 83200

march 20, 2010

mr. Thomas ramsey

the trading Card company

603 N. shane Ln.

travis City, Co 81120

dear Mr. Ramsey:

Thank you for sending the Tyreik Taylor trading card so

quickly. Unfortunately, it is not the item that I ordered. I

am returning it in this envelope. Please send the Vaughn

Vernon card by return mail. If the Vaughn Vernon card

is not available, please enclose a refund check.

yours truly,

shane caldwell

 ERRORS: MAKE UPPERCASE: 17

23 Ordering a Scarf Kit

453 mayfield Rd.

Artville, Ab T0R 0V3

february 3, 2010

Ms. veronica Shelby

old town Yarn shop

325 W. ramsey Blvd.

owensville, On K3W 0F6

dear ms. shelby:

I would like to order the wool scarf kit that you

advertised in the January issue of Teen Knits Magazine.

Red is my first choice, but if that is unavailable, blue

would be fine. I have enclosed a check for the full

amount. I look forward to receiving my kit.

sincerely yours,

Wendy thomas

ERRORS: MAKE UPPERCASE: 16

Name: _____ Date: _____

24 Trading Card Mix-Up

154 s. Garrett ct.

pleasanton, Id 83200

march 20, 2010

mr. Thomas ramsey

the trading Card company

603 N. shane Ln.

travis City, Co 81120

dear Mr. Ramsey:

Thank you for sending the Tyreik Taylor trading card so

quickly. Unfortunately, it is not the item that I ordered. I

am returning it in this envelope. Please send the Vaughn

Vernon card by return mail. If the Vaughn Vernon card

is not available, please enclose a refund check.

yours truly,

shane caldwell

Name: _____ Date: _____

23 Ordering a Scarf Kit

453 mayfield Rd.

Artville, Ab T0R 0V3

february 3, 2010

ms. veronica Shelby

old town Yarn shop

325 W. ramsey Blvd.

owensville, On K3W 0F6

dear ms. shelby:

I would like to order the wool scarf kit that you

advertised in the January issue of Teen Knits Magazine.

Red is my first choice, but if that is unavailable, blue

would be fine. I have enclosed a check for the full

amount. I look forward to receiving my kit.

sincerely yours,

Wendy thomas

25 Toronto Publications

I visited my uncle in Toronto last summer. He is a journalist. He writes a column for the toronto star. Most people just call his paper the star. It is Toronto's largest daily newspaper. I found out that there are several other newspapers in the city. The two largest are the toronto sun and the toronto free press. Toronto also has its own magazines. They include toronto life and eye magazine. After my uncle gave me a tour of the newspaper office, my aunt found the name of a great restaurant in her copy of today's parent: toronto families.

ERRORS: MAKE UPPERCASE: 16

26 Favorite Magazines

Our library has an excellent periodicals room. Its shelves are stocked with magazines for all ages and interests. David, my best friend, likes to read boys' life. Janice, my sister, likes american girl. Krista, my three-year-old niece, loves the animal pictures in your big backyard. My older brother, Jason, is interested in the news, so he reads faze magazine. Anna, my neighbor, had a poem published in stone soup last month. Larry, our school's science wizard, reads odyssey: Adventures in science, owl, and national wildlife. I love geography, so national Geographic world is my favorite magazine.

ERRORS: MAKE UPPERCASE: 18

Name: _____ Date: _____

Toronto Publications (25)

I visited my uncle in Toronto last summer. He is a journalist. He writes a column for the toronto star. Most people just call his paper the star. It is Toronto's largest daily newspaper. I found out that there are several other newspapers in the city. The two largest are the toronto sun and the toronto free press. Toronto also has its own magazines. They include toronto life and eye magazine. After my uncle gave me a tour of the newspaper office, my aunt found the name of a great restaurant in her copy of today's parent: toronto families.

✔ LOOK FOR: NAMES OF MAGAZINES AND NEWSPAPERS

Name: _____ Date: _____

Favorite Magazines (26)

Our library has an excellent periodicals room. Its shelves are stocked with magazines for all ages and interests. David, my best friend, likes to read boys' life. Janice, my sister, likes american girl. Krista, my three-year-old niece, loves the animal pictures in your big backyard. My older brother, Jason, is interested in the news, so he reads faze magazine. Anna, my neighbor, had a poem published in stone soup last month. Larry, our school's science wizard, reads odyssey: Adventures in science, owl, and national wildlife. I love geography, so national Geographic world is my favorite magazine.

✔ LOOK FOR: NAMES OF MAGAZINES

27 The Martinville Service Society

Our service club, the martinville service society, is collecting money for the dustin evans memorial children's fund. Dustin was a member of our group for more than a year. He always wanted to go to summer camp, but his parents could not afford to send him. After Dustin passed away last year, our sponsor helped us set up the fund. It will provide camp scholarships to deserving fourth and fifth graders. We are writing letters to local businesses asking them to contribute. So far, martinville music store has donated the most, but the owners of clarke's plumbing service and chelsea's main street salon have also been generous.

ERRORS: MAKE UPPERCASE: 18

28 Bad Plumbing

Last month, our kitchen drain was clogged, so Mom called bart's plumbing and heating service. Unfortunately, the plumber they sent did not do a very good job. He failed to clear the drain, and he left a mess on the floor. The company would not send anyone else, so Mom called abe's dandy drain service. Abe came himself. He cleared the drain quickly, and he even cleaned up the mess. He told Mom to report bart's to the city's better business bureau. As soon as Abe left, Mom followed his advice. She also called the society of plumbing engineers. They assured her that they would investigate the problem.

ERRORS: MAKE UPPERCASE: 15

Name: _____ Date: _____

The Martinville Service Society   27

Our service club, the martinville service society, is collecting money for the dustin

evans memorial children's fund. Dustin was a member of our group for more than a

year. He always wanted to go to summer camp, but his parents could not afford to

send him. After Dustin passed away last year, our sponsor helped us set up the fund.

It will provide camp scholarships to deserving fourth and fifth graders. We are writing

letters to local businesses asking them to contribute. So far, martinville music store has

donated the most, but the owners of clarke's plumbing service and chelsea's main

street salon have also been generous.

✔ LOOK FOR: NAMES OF ORGANIZATIONS AND BUSINESSES

Name: _____ Date: _____

Bad Plumbing   28

Last month, our kitchen drain was clogged, so Mom called bart's plumbing and

heating service. Unfortunately, the plumber they sent did not do a very good job. He

failed to clear the drain, and he left a mess on the floor. The company would not send

anyone else, so Mom called abe's dandy drain service. Abe came himself. He cleared

the drain quickly, and he even cleaned up the mess. He told Mom to report bart's

to the city's better business bureau. As soon as Abe left, Mom followed his advice.

She also called the society of plumbing engineers. They assured her that they would

investigate the problem.

✔ LOOK FOR: NAMES OF ORGANIZATIONS AND BUSINESSES

29 Van Gogh's Self-Portraits

A portrait is a picture of a person or a special animal, such as a racehorse or a family pet. Many artists have portrayed themselves in their work. Such paintings, drawings, or photographic prints are called *self-portraits*. Between 1886 and 1888, the painter Vincent van Gogh created more than 20 expressive self-portraits. They include self-portrait with dark felt hat, Self-portrait with dark felt hat at the easel, self-Portrait with pipe, Self-Portrait with straw Hat and pipe, Self-Portrait with a japanese print, and Self-portrait in Front of the easel.

 ERRORS: MAKE UPPERCASE: 18

30 Variations on a Theme

Composers use many different forms to create their music. One of these forms uses a musical theme with variations. At the beginning of this type of piece, the composer introduces a musical phrase. In the rest of the composition, he changes that phrase in as many ways as possible. He makes it faster or slower, louder or softer, and he changes its rhythm. He rearranges the notes of the phrase, sometimes reversing their order, and he uses different instruments to accompany it. Sergei Rachmaninoff's rhapsody on a theme of paganini, Edward Elgar's enigma variations, Johann Sebastian Bach's goldberg variations, and Arnold Schoenberg's variations for orchestra are famous examples of this form. Benjamin Britten's composition The young person's guide to the orchestra is also such a work.

ERRORS: MAKE UPPERCASE: 13

Name: _____ Date: _____

Van Gogh's Self-Portraits (29)

A portrait is a picture of a person or a special animal, such as a racehorse or a family pet. Many artists have portrayed themselves in their work. Such paintings, drawings, or photographic prints are called *self-portraits*. Between 1886 and 1888, the painter Vincent van Gogh created more than 20 expressive self-portraits. They include self-portrait with dark felt hat, Self-portrait with dark felt hat at the easel, self-Portrait with pipe, Self-Portrait with straw Hat and pipe, Self-Portrait with a japanese print, and Self-portrait in Front of the easel.

LOOK FOR: NAMES OF WORKS OF ART

Name: _____ Date: _____

Variations on a Theme (30)

Composers use many different forms to create their music. One of these forms uses a musical theme with variations. At the beginning of this type of piece, the composer introduces a musical phrase. In the rest of the composition, he changes that phrase in as many ways as possible. He makes it faster or slower, louder or softer, and he changes its rhythm. He rearranges the notes of the phrase, sometimes reversing their order, and he uses different instruments to accompany it. Sergei Rachmaninoff's rhapsody on a theme of paganini, Edward Elgar's enigma variations, Johann Sebastian Bach's goldberg variations, and Arnold Schoenberg's variations for orchestra are famous examples of this form. Benjamin Britten's composition The young person's guide to the orchestra is also such a work.

LOOK FOR: NAMES OF MUSICAL COMPOSITIONS

31 Art Appreciation

453 logan Ave.

Heathton, MB R2E 0H6

october 15, 2010

mr. Byron Shelby, Editor

delaney star

552 Hugo blvd.

macon, On K3W 0F6

dear mr. Shelby:

I read your editorial in last Monday's paper. I agree

that we are lucky to have Marcella Nassim's painting

blue pier at the macon Art gallery. Different people

enjoy different kinds of art. Thank you for defending the

exhibition and the sponsor, downtown music and books.

sincerely,

gene Madison

32 Listening to Beethoven

306 N. Austin rd.

sunnydale, Az 85001

may 12, 2010

Mr. Robert ashton

sunnydale Performing arts Complex

322 W. camden Terr.

sunnydale, aZ 85001

dear Mr. Ashton:

Thank you for visiting our class. I enjoyed hearing

Beethoven's music. The moonlight sonata was

beautiful. I read an article about your next

performance in the sunnydale life Magazine. I look

forward to hearing you play at the concert for the

arizona children's society next weekend.

sincerely yours,

Maddie Carvalle

Name: _____ Date: _____

32 Listening to Beethoven

306 N. Austin rd.

sunnydale, Az 85001

may 12, 2010

Mr. Robert ashton

sunnydale Performing arts Complex

322 W. camden Terr.

sunnydale, aZ 85001

dear Mr. Ashton:

Thank you for visiting our class. I enjoyed hearing

Beethoven's music. The <u>moonlight sonata</u> was

beautiful. I read an article about your next

performance in the <u>sunnydale life Magazine</u>. I look

forward to hearing you play at the concert for the

arizona children's society next weekend.

sincerely yours,

Maddie Carvalle

Name: _____ Date: _____

31 Art Appreciation

453 logan Ave.

Heathton, MB R2E 0H6

october 15, 2010

mr. Byron Shelby, Editor

<u>delaney star</u>

552 Hugo blvd.

macon, On K3W 0F6

dear mr. Shelby:

I read your editorial in last Monday's paper. I agree

that we are lucky to have Marcella Nassim's painting

<u>blue pier</u> at the macon Art gallery. Different people

enjoy different kinds of art. Thank you for defending the

exhibition and the sponsor, downtown music and books.

sincerely,

gene Madison

33 ### A Weekend in the Woods

Hannah was standing on her porch when the phone rang. She ran to answer it.

"hello?" she said.

"hi, Hannah. It's Jordana. Are you ready?" she asked.

"yes, I am waiting outside," Hannah said.

"we will be there in five minutes. Did you pack a swimsuit?" Jordana asked.

"do I need one?" Hannah asked.

"yes, there is a lake near the cabin," Jordana said.

"that sounds like fun, but I don't have a suit," Hannah said.

"i have an extra one that you can wear," Jordana said.

"great!" Hannah said.

ERRORS: MAKE UPPERCASE: 9

---

 34 ### A Close Call

Nathan was running as fast as he could. When he caught up with Brad, he was out of breath. "i have to tell you something," he panted.

Brad sat down on a nearby park bench. "come over here and sit down," he said.

Nathan also sat on the bench. "guess what happened to Edgar Dennis," he said.

Brad's eyes were wide with curiosity. "what?!" he asked.

Nathan leaned toward Brad. "he was running, and he tripped over a bench," he said.

Brad looked concerned. "was he hurt?" he asked.

"the principal called the paramedics," Nathan said. "they told all of us to go home."

"is he all right?" Brad asked worriedly.

"i think he is," Nathan said. "he was sitting on a bench when I left, and he waved to me."

ERRORS: MAKE UPPERCASE: 11

Name: _____ Date: _____

A Weekend in the Woods (33)

Hannah was standing on her porch when the phone rang. She ran to answer it.

"hello?" she said.

"hi, Hannah. It's Jordana. Are you ready?" she asked.

"yes, I am waiting outside," Hannah said.

"we will be there in five minutes. Did you pack a swimsuit?" Jordana asked.

"do I need one?" Hannah asked.

"yes, there is a lake near the cabin," Jordana said.

"that sounds like fun, but I don't have a suit," Hannah said.

"i have an extra one that you can wear," Jordana said.

"great!" Hannah said.

✔ LOOK FOR: FIRST WORD IN A DIRECT QUOTATION

Name: _____ Date: _____

A Close Call (34)

Nathan was running as fast as he could. When he caught up with Brad, he was out of breath. "i have to tell you something," he panted.

Brad sat down on a nearby park bench. "come over here and sit down," he said.

Nathan also sat on the bench. "guess what happened to Edgar Dennis," he said.

Brad's eyes were wide with curiosity. "what?!" he asked.

Nathan leaned toward Brad. "he was running, and he tripped over a bench," he said.

Brad looked concerned. "was he hurt?" he asked.

"the principal called the paramedics," Nathan said. "they told all of us to go home."

"is he all right?" Brad asked worriedly.

"i think he is," Nathan said. "he was sitting on a bench when I left, and he waved to me."

✔ LOOK FOR: FIRST WORD IN A DIRECT QUOTATION

36 An Interesting Exhibit

500 W. Kenyon ln.

Oakton, al 35199

March 9, 2010

Dr. Clayton Holley, director of Exhibitions

Oakton Art museum

445 Carson blvd.

oakton, AL 35199

dear dr. Holley:

Today, my Mom and I toured the museum's latest exhibit. We agreed with the quote in Saturday's oakton tribune. It said, "this exhibit is like a time machine." My favorite photograph was of an irish family from the great Depression. I also liked the painting of the tigers baseball team called strikeout. Thank you for choosing this exhibit.

sincerely,

Shane Patrick

35 Fascinating Reading

I picked up the latest issue of Around the world when I was at the dentist's office last week. First, I read an article about the absence of land plants during the cambrian period of the paleozoic era. Then, I read an article by Ned Clive of the world Relief society about the indonesian earthquake. It was hard for the volunteers to communicate because some spoke japanese, some spoke english, and some spoke Dutch. Despite this challenge, the way that the christian, Jewish, and muslim groups worked together to help the victims was inspiring. I had just started an article about planets when the hygienist called me. After the appointment, mom took me to Bob's corner Mart to buy my own copy of the magazine. I finished reading about venus and mars. Next, I want to read the article about the composer Vivaldi's masterpiece, The four seasons, and finally, the article about hiking trails in the Pacific northwest.

Name: _____ Date: _____

35 Fascinating Reading

I picked up the latest issue of Around the world when I

was at the dentist's office last week. First, I read an article

about the absence of land plants during the cambrian

period of the paleozoic era. Then, I read an article by

Ned Clive of the world Relief society about the indonesian

earthquake. It was hard for the volunteers to communicate

because some spoke japanese, some spoke english, and

some spoke Dutch. Despite this challenge, the way that

the christian, Jewish, and muslim groups worked together

to help the victims was inspiring. I had just started an article

about planets when the hygienist called me. After the

appointment, mom took me to Bob's corner Mart to buy

my own copy of the magazine. I finished reading about

venus and mars. Next, I want to read the article about the

composer Vivaldi's masterpiece, The four seasons, and

finally, the article about hiking trails in the Pacific northwest.

CUMULATIVE REVIEW

Name: _____ Date: _____

36 An Interesting Exhibit

500 W. Kenyon ln.

Oakton, aL 35199

March 9, 2010

Dr. Clayton Holley, director of Exhibitions

Oakton Art museum

445 Carson blvd.

oakton, AL 35199

dear dr. Holley:

Today, my Mom and I toured the museum's latest

exhibit. We agreed with the quote in Saturday's oakton

tribune. It said, "this exhibit is like a time machine." My

favorite photograph was of an irish family from the great

Depression. I also liked the painting of the tigers baseball

team called strikeout. Thank you for choosing this exhibit.

sincerely,

Shane Patrick

CUMULATIVE REVIEW

37 Graphite Pencils

Because the ancient Greeks and Romans sometimes used thin lead rods for drawing, we call the core of today's pencil a "lead." Actually, a pencil's lead contains no lead at all. Instead, it is made from a mixture of graphite and clay. Graphite, a form of carbon, is a soft, black mineral. In its natural form, graphite is greasy to the touch. Because it marked surfaces easily, the mineral's discoverer, the German geologist Abraham Werner, gave it a name derived from the Greek word meaning "to write." Although graphite deposits are common, there are not many graphite mines. Most of the graphite we use is manufactured from coke, a product formed when coal is heated in an airtight oven.

ERRORS: PERIODS: 8

38 Plate Tectonics

Earth's crust is broken into huge pieces called *tectonic plates*. These plates include whole continents and sections of the ocean floor. Tectonic plates are shifting constantly. The uneven line where two plates meet is called a *rift zone*. Earthquakes often occur along rift zones. When part of a slowly moving plate sticks to an opposing plate at a point along the rift zone, pressure builds. The pressure rises behind the stubborn section until finally it gives way and moves. The shock from this sudden shift is like a stone tossed into a pond. It sends out waves in all directions. These waves travel through layers of rock in the same way that ocean waves travel through water. If buildings are on top of the land, they will shake as an earthquake wave passes by.

ERRORS: PERIODS: 11

Name: _____ Date: _____

Graphite Pencils (37)

Because the ancient Greeks and Romans sometimes used thin lead rods for drawing, we call the core of today's pencil a "lead." Actually, a pencil's lead contains no lead at all Instead, it is made from a mixture of graphite and clay Graphite, a form of carbon, is a soft, black mineral In its natural form, graphite is greasy to the touch Because it marked surfaces easily, the mineral's discoverer, the German geologist Abraham Werner, gave it a name derived from the Greek word meaning "to write" Although graphite deposits are common, there are not many graphite mines Most of the graphite we use is manufactured from coke, a product formed when coal is heated in an airtight oven

✔ LOOK FOR: SENTENCE ENDINGS

Name: _____ Date: _____

Plate Tectonics (38)

Earth's crust is broken into huge pieces called *tectonic plates* These plates include whole continents and sections of the ocean floor Tectonic plates are shifting constantly The uneven line where two plates meet is called a *rift zone* Earthquakes often occur along rift zones When part of a slowly moving plate sticks to an opposing plate at a point along the rift zone, pressure builds The pressure rises behind the stubborn section until finally it gives way and moves The shock from this sudden shift is like a stone tossed into a pond It sends out waves in all directions These waves travel through layers of rock in the same way that ocean waves travel through water If buildings are on top of the land, they will shake as an earthquake wave passes by

✔ LOOK FOR: SENTENCE ENDINGS

39 The Milky Way Galaxy

The Milky Way is our galaxy¸a galaxy is a large group of stars. There are more than 200 billion stars in the Milky Way¸our sun is one of them. The Milky Way is not the only galaxy¸there are about 30 galaxies in the Local Group alone. The Local Group is part of a cluster¸the cluster includes about 3,000 galaxies. There are many other clusters of galaxies in the universe¸the Great Wall of galaxies is approximately 15 million light years thick. Scientists estimate that there are billions of galaxies like our own in space¸many are visible through a telescope. Some of them, like the Milky Way, have a spiral shape¸others are elliptical, irregular, or barred spirals.

ERRORS: SEMICOLONS: 7

40 Reindeer

Although more widely known as characters in fiction, reindeer are real animals¸they live in North America, Europe, and Asia. Both male and female reindeer have large antlers¸these impressive weapons help protect them from hungry grizzly bears and wolves. They have wider hooves than other deer¸their special hooves help them walk in the snow and uncover buried lichens. Reindeer herds migrate across marshes and tundra near the Arctic Circle¸they must move frequently to follow their food supply. Not all reindeer are wild in Scandinavia¸the Sami people have tamed them. They use the large deer to pull sleighs¸they even drink reindeer milk. In some places, people use modern equipment to help reindeer¸they guide and protect their herds with snowmobiles or helicopters.

ERRORS: SEMICOLONS: 7

Name: _____ Date: _____

The Milky Way Galaxy (39)

The Milky Way is our galaxy a galaxy is a large group of stars. There are more than 200 billion stars in the Milky Way our sun is one of them. The Milky Way is not the only galaxy there are about 30 galaxies in the Local Group alone. The Local Group is part of a cluster the cluster includes about 3,000 galaxies. There are many other clusters of galaxies in the universe the Great Wall of galaxies is approximately 15 million light years thick. Scientists estimate that there are billions of galaxies like our own in space many are visible through a telescope. Some of them, like the Milky Way, have a spiral shape others are elliptical, irregular, or barred spirals.

✔ LOOK FOR: INDEPENDENT CLAUSES

Name: _____ Date: _____

Reindeer (40)

Although more widely known as characters in fiction, reindeer are real animals they live in North America, Europe, and Asia. Both male and female reindeer have large antlers these impressive weapons help protect them from hungry grizzly bears and wolves. They have wider hooves than other deer their special hooves help them walk in the snow and uncover buried lichens. Reindeer herds migrate across marshes and tundra near the Arctic Circle they must move frequently to follow their food supply. Not all reindeer are wild in Scandinavia the Sami people have tamed them. They use the large deer to pull sleighs they even drink reindeer milk. In some places, people use modern equipment to help reindeer they guide and protect their herds with snowmobiles or helicopters.

✔ LOOK FOR: INDEPENDENT CLAUSES

Thur

41 Rock Hound Excursion

670 Zane Place

Copperton, NB E2Z 0R4

May 9, 2010

Dr. Zabrea Williams

Crystal Rock Shop

708 Lawrence Ave.

Copperton, NB E2Z 0R4

Dear Dr. Williams:

Thank you for inviting our rock hound club to your shop.

We will arrive at 2:00 or 2:15 P.M. next Saturday afternoon.

My father will pick us up at 3:30 or 3:45 P.M. We would like

to see the following rocks: quartz crystals, fool's gold, and

copper ore. Our club includes the following members:

Porchia, Owen, Tyler, and me. We are looking forward to

our visit.

Sincerely,
Warren Xavier

ERRORS: COLONS: 7

42 Looking for Books

213 N. Owen Dr.

Middletown, OH 43222

April 23, 2010

Mr. Patrick Ryan

Quiet Corner Used Books

530 Reese Blvd.

Sierra City, NV 68002

Dear Mr. Ryan:

My mother and I are looking for the following books:

Amazing Rescues by George Shea, The Secret Garden by

Frances Hodgson Burnett, and Stuart Little by E. B. White.

My mom would like to talk to you about the following

details: prices, available editions, and similar books. She

works from 9:30 A.M. to 6:00 P.M. each weekday. Are you

open at 7:00 in the evening or before 9:00 in the morning?

Sincerely yours,
Sandra Quinton

ERRORS: COLONS: 7

Name: _____ Date: _____

41 Rock Hound Excursion

670 Zane Place

Copperton, NB E2Z 0R4

May 9, 2010

Dr. Zabrea Williams

Crystal Rock Shop

708 Lawrence Ave.

Copperton, NB E2Z 0R4

Dear Dr. Williams

Thank you for inviting our rock hound club to your shop.

We will arrive at 200 or 215 P.M. next Saturday afternoon.

My father will pick us up at 330 or 345 P.M. We would like

to see the following rocks quartz crystals, fool's gold, and

copper ore. Our club includes the following members

Porchia, Owen, Tyler, and me. We are looking forward to

our visit.

Sincerely,
Warren Xavier

✔ LOOK FOR: BUSINESS LETTER GREETINGS, LISTS, & TIMES

Name: _____ Date: _____

42 Looking for Books

213 N. Owen Dr.

Middletown, OH 43222

April 23, 2010

Mr. Patrick Ryan

Quiet Corner Used Books

530 Reese Blvd.

Sierra City, NV 68002

Dear Mr. Ryan

My mother and I are looking for the following books

Amazing Rescues by George Shea, The Secret Garden by

Frances Hodgson Burnett, and Stuart Little by E. B. White.

My mom would like to talk to you about the following

details prices, available editions, and similar books. She

works from 930 A.M. to 600 P.M. each weekday. Are you

open at 700 in the evening or before 900 in the morning?

Sincerely yours,
Sandra Quinton

✔ LOOK FOR: BUSINESS LETTER GREETINGS, LISTS, & TIMES

Animal Shelter Adoption Drive

To: clarissa@nomail.zap
From: audreydesandro@nomail.zap

Dear Clarissa,

Here is a quick reminder the animal shelter's adoption drive is this Saturday Thank you for signing up We will need help at the following times 830 A.M. to 930 A.M., 1230 P.M. to 130 P.M., and 330 P.M. to 430 P.M. Please call as soon as possible we want to add you to our schedule We will provide the following water, snacks, and lunch Please bring the following sunscreen, insect repellent, and a hat Plan to arrive at least one-half hour before your scheduled time check in at the front desk Ms. Cameron will give you a badge See you Saturday!

Sincerely,
Audrey Desandro, Director

ERRORS: PERIODS: 7; SEMICOLONS: 2; COLONS: 10

Thank-You Letter Help

To: justin@nomail.zap
From: carson@nomail.zap

Dear Justin,

Mrs. Carter asked me to write a letter to the fire department she wants me to thank the firefighters for attending Career Day They gave an excellent presentation. I especially enjoyed the following their stories about dramatic rescues, their truck, and the protective gear they wore Can you think of anything else I should include? I hope you can help me with something else too I am trying to remember what time the firefighters spoke it was either 115 or 215 I have to write the letter by 300 call me as soon as you can.

Your friend,
Carson

ERRORS: PERIODS: 4; SEMICOLONS: 3; COLONS: 4

Name: _____   Date: _____

Animal Shelter Adoption Drive 〔43〕

To: clarissa@nomail.zap
From: audreydesandro@nomail.zap

Dear Clarissa,

Here is a quick reminder the animal shelter's adoption drive is this Saturday Thank you for signing up We will need help at the following times 830 A.M. to 930 A.M., 1230 P.M. to 130 P.M., and 330 P.M. to 430 P.M. Please call as soon as possible we want to add you to our schedule We will provide the following water, snacks, and lunch Please bring the following sunscreen, insect repellent, and a hat Plan to arrive at least one-half hour before your scheduled time check in at the front desk Ms. Cameron will give you a badge See you Saturday!

Sincerely,
Audrey Desandro, Director

✔ MIXED REVIEW

Name: _____   Date: _____

Thank-You Letter Help 〔44〕

To: justin@nomail.zap
From: carson@nomail.zap

Dear Justin,

Mrs. Carter asked me to write a letter to the fire department she wants me to thank the firefighters for attending Career Day They gave an excellent presentation. I especially enjoyed the following their stories about dramatic rescues, their truck, and the protective gear they wore Can you think of anything else I should include? I hope you can help me with something else too I am trying to remember what time the firefighters spoke it was either 115 or 215 I have to write the letter by 300 call me as soon as you can.

Your friend,
Carson

✔ MIXED REVIEW

45 Cereal Fractions

Today, we learned about equivalent fractions. Our group counted pieces of cereal.

We separated our pieces into equal groups. It is a well-known fact that six-eighths
                                                                ∧   ∧
is equivalent to three-fourths. We discovered other fractions that are equivalent
                        ∧
to three-fourths. They are nine-twelfths, twelve-sixteenths, fifteen-twentieths, and
         ∧   ∧   ∧   ∧
eighteen-twenty-fourths. If we had more cereal, we could have modeled many more
        ∧   ∧
equivalent fractions.

ERRORS: HYPHENS: 9

46 My Sister's Wedding

Last Saturday, my oldest sister married her boyfriend. Now, I have a brother-in-law. My
                                                                            ∧ ∧
uncle says that he is a know-it-all. Dad does not like him, but my sister loves him. That
                            ∧∧
is all that matters. I met three-quarters of his family at the wedding. The others were
                              ∧
not able to come. We spent one-third of the afternoon waiting for everyone to arrive.
                             ∧
The ceremony was not very long. Afterward, there was a big dinner. The photographer

took a close-up of me. I ate only one-sixth of my dinner. I was not very hungry. I was
           ∧   ∧
too excited. This weekend, Mom, Dad, and I will have a follow-up celebration at my
                                                              ∧
great-uncle's cabin. It should be very peaceful. Mom and Dad say that they need a
     ∧
good rest.

ERRORS: HYPHENS: 10

Name: _____ Date: _____

Cereal Fractions (45) ✓

Today, we learned about equivalent fractions. Our group counted pieces of cereal. We separated our pieces into equal groups. It is a well known fact that six eighths is equivalent to three fourths. We discovered other fractions that are equivalent to three fourths. They are nine twelfths, twelve sixteenths, fifteen twentieths, and eighteen twenty fourths. If we had more cereal, we could have modeled many more equivalent fractions.

✔ LOOK FOR: FRACTIONS AND COMPOUND MODIFIERS

Name: _____ Date: _____

My Sister's Wedding (46) ✓

Last Saturday, my oldest sister married her boyfriend. Now, I have a brother in law. My uncle says that he is a know it all. Dad does not like him, but my sister loves him. That is all that matters. I met three quarters of his family at the wedding. The others were not able to come. We spent one third of the afternoon waiting for everyone to arrive. The ceremony was not very long. Afterward, there was a big dinner. The photographer took a close up of me. I ate only one sixth of my dinner. I was not very hungry. I was too excited. This weekend, Mom, Dad, and I will have a follow up celebration at my great uncle's cabin. It should be very peaceful. Mom and Dad say that they need a good rest.

✔ LOOK FOR: FRACTIONS AND COMPOUND NOUNS AND MODIFIERS

47 Family Gathering

Our family had a get together last week. I met Great Aunt Carrie for the first time. She
took my younger brother and me to the park. My brother rode on the merry go round. I
wish I had one of those life size horses in my room. After leaving the park, we went to the
mall. Great Aunt Carrie took away my worn out sweater. She bought me a brand new
one. Great Aunt Carrie left on Sunday. She was hurrying home to host a fund raiser for a
hospital in her town. I hope she visits us again soon.

✗ ERRORS: HYPHENS: 10

48 My Mom's Business

My mom has a home based business. She sells award winning, popular products. Her
business started as a part time job. Now, it is a full time, full scale operation. Mom is
old fashioned. She does not like to rely on babysitters. She wanted to stay home with
my two year old sister. Now, she has long range plans for making more sales. Last
month, she bought an up to date computer system. All of us are proud of her.

✗ ERRORS: HYPHENS: 11

Name: _____   Date: _____

Family Gathering   47

Our family had a get together last week. I met Great Aunt Carrie for the first time. She took my younger brother and me to the park. My brother rode on the merry go round. I wish I had one of those life size horses in my room. After leaving the park, we went to the mall. Great Aunt Carrie took away my worn out sweater. She bought me a brand new one. Great Aunt Carrie left on Sunday. She was hurrying home to host a fund raiser for a hospital in her town. I hope she visits us again soon.

✔ **LOOK FOR: COMPOUND NOUNS AND MODIFIERS**

Name: _____   Date: _____

My Mom's Business   48

My mom has a home based business. She sells award winning, popular products. Her business started as a part time job. Now, it is a full time, full scale operation. Mom is old fashioned. She does not like to rely on babysitters. She wanted to stay home with my two year old sister. Now, she has long range plans for making more sales. Last month, she bought an up to date computer system. All of us are proud of her.

✔ **LOOK FOR: COMPOUND MODIFIERS**

Girls' Club

Our next club get-together will be on Saturday. The following girls have been invited:

Sabena, Yolanda, Patrice, Sadie, and Wynona. Yolanda is our only Spanish-speaking

member. Of course, I will be there too. We need the following supplies: a well-made

quilt, three-fourths cups of cheese crackers, a jack-in-the-box, paper cups, one and

one-half gallons of juice drink, and six V-neck T-shirts. I am excited because our club is

becoming popular so quickly. People have heard about it only by word-of-mouth, but

five-sixths of the girls in our class have asked to join. So far, the club has been very

time-consuming but well worth the effort.

ERRORS: HYPHENS: 14

 At the Doctor's Office

On Wednesday, two-thirds of the doctor's patients arrived before check-in time. The

remaining one-third arrived on time or late. Keon, a 10-year-old, arrived on time for his

appointment. His great-uncle drove him to the appointment. Keon needed to get an

X-ray of his leg. It had been hurting him since he landed on it while playing basketball

the night before. He hoped that his leg wasn't broken. He also hoped that his

appointment didn't take more than one and one-fourth hours. His fifth-grade teacher

was giving a math test that afternoon, and he didn't want to make it up later. After

waiting for twenty-two minutes, a middle-aged nurse finally called Keon's name.

ERRORS: HYPHENS: 11

Name: _____ Date: _____

Girls' Club (49)

Our next club get together will be on Saturday. The following girls have been invited: Sabena, Yolanda, Patrice, Sadie, and Wynona. Yolanda is our only Spanish speaking member. Of course, I will be there too. We need the following supplies: a well made quilt, three fourths cups of cheese crackers, a jack in the box, paper cups, one and one half gallons of juice drink, and six V neck T shirts. I am excited because our club is becoming popular so quickly. People have heard about it only by word of mouth, but five sixths of the girls in our class have asked to join. So far, the club has been very time consuming but well worth the effort.

✔ MIXED REVIEW

Name: _____ Date: _____

At the Doctor's Office (50)

On Wednesday, two thirds of the doctor's patients arrived before check in time. The remaining one third arrived on time or late. Keon, a 10 year old, arrived on time for his appointment. His great uncle drove him to the appointment. Keon needed to get an X ray of his leg. It had been hurting him since he landed on it while playing basketball the night before. He hoped that his leg wasn't broken. He also hoped that his appointment didn't take more than one and one fourth hours. His fifth grade teacher was giving a math test that afternoon, and he didn't want to make it up later. After waiting for twenty two minutes, a middle aged nurse finally called Keon's name.

✔ MIXED REVIEW

52 Protecting the Forests

114 W. Hampden Ct.

Eastville, CA 95555

Oct. 27, 2010

Sen. Darrell V. Jones

100 Hart Senate Office Building

Washington, DC 20510

Dear Senator Jones:

Thank you for voting for the Forest Protection Act. I

enjoy spending time in the woods with my family. We

hike and camp every summer. Now, the forests will be

saved for my children and their children. We are lucky

to have you as our senator.

Sincerely yours,

Virginia Kinkade

ERRORS: COMMAS: 4

51 Protecting Animals

689 Terrance Way

Williamston, ON K5R 2S8

June 1, 2010

Sen. Richard Whitney

The Senate of Canada

Ottawa, ON K1A 0A4

Dear Sen. Whitney:

Thank you for supporting the endangered animals

law. My parents and I love to see animals in the wild.

Someday, my children will enjoy them too. I will tell

them the story of this law. Then, they will understand

that caring people can have an impact on the world

around them.

Yours truly,

Wayne Phillips

ERRORS: COMMAS: 4

Name: _____ Date: _____

51 Protecting Animals

689 Terrance Way

Williamston ON K5R 2S8

June 1 2010

Sen. Richard Whitney

The Senate of Canada

Ottawa ON K1A 0A4

Dear Sen. Whitney:

Thank you for supporting the endangered animals

law. My parents and I love to see animals in the wild. We

Someday, my children will enjoy them too. I will tell

them the story of this law. Then, they will understand

that caring people can have an impact on the world

around them.

Yours truly

Wayne Phillips

Name: _____ Date: _____

52 Protecting the Forests

114 W. Hampden Ct.

Eastville CA 95555

Oct. 27 2010

Sen. Darrell V. Jones

100 Hart Senate Office Building

Washington DC 20510

Dear Senator Jones:

Thank you for voting for the Forest Protection Act. I

enjoy spending time in the woods with my family. We

hike and camp every summer. Now, the forests will be

saved for my children and their children. We are lucky

to have you as our senator.

Sincerely yours

Virginia Kinkade

Model Airplane

To: stephen@nomail.zap
From: tony@nomail.zap

Dear Stephen,

Well, I am still working on the model airplane that you gave me. Yes, it is hard, but I am determined to finish. First, I tried to fit one wing into a slot on the body. Of course, I pinched my finger. Ow, that hurt. Well, I dashed right into the bathroom. I held my finger under cold running water. Ah, that felt good. Next, I spilled glue all over the table. Wow, what a mess! I am feeling slightly discouraged, but I will not give up! My brother will help me with the plane later. Hey, I am really looking forward to hanging that model in my room.

Your friend,
Tony

ERRORS: COMMAS: 10

 Zoe's New Camera

"Hi," Zoe said as she opened her front door. Her friend Jasmine had arrived.

"Whew, I am out of breath," Jasmine gasped.

"Yikes, did you run all of the way here?" Zoe asked.

"Hey, you said to hurry," Jasmine said.

"Yes, I wanted to show you my new camera," Zoe said.

"Wow, your dad really bought you a camera?!" Jasmine exclaimed incredulously.

"Absolutely, it is right here," Zoe said. She picked up the camera and focused it on her friend. "Smile, you are famous!" she said as she pressed the button.

"Oops, I might have blinked," Jasmine said.

"Oh, that's not a problem," Zoe said. "I will just take another one."

ERRORS: COMMAS: 9

Name: _____ Date: _____

Model Airplane 53

To: stephen@nomail.zap
From: tony@nomail.zap

Dear Stephen,

Well I am still working on the model airplane that you gave me. Yes it is hard, but I am determined to finish. First I tried to fit one wing into a slot on the body. Of course I pinched my finger. Ow that hurt. Well I dashed right into the bathroom. I held my finger under cold running water. Ah that felt good. Next I spilled glue all over the table. Wow what a mess! I am feeling slightly discouraged, but I will not give up! My brother will help me with the plane later. Hey I am really looking forward to hanging that model in my room.

Your friend,
Tony

✔ LOOK FOR: INTERJECTIONS AND INTRODUCTORY WORDS AND PHRASES

Name: _____ Date: _____

Zoe's New Camera 54

"Hi," Zoe said as she opened her front door. Her friend Jasmine had arrived.

"Whew I am out of breath," Jasmine gasped.

"Yikes did you run all of the way here?" Zoe asked.

"Hey you said to hurry," Jasmine said.

"Yes I wanted to show you my new camera," Zoe said.

"Wow your dad really bought you a camera?!" Jasmine exclaimed incredulously.

"Absolutely it is right here," Zoe said. She picked up the camera and focused it on her friend. "Smile you are famous!" she said as she pressed the button.

"Oops I might have blinked," Jasmine said.

"Oh that's not a problem," Zoe said. "I will just take another one."

✔ LOOK FOR: INTERJECTIONS AND INTRODUCTORY WORDS AND PHRASES

55 Children's Book Week

Our class is celebrating Children's Book Week. We made a chart. It lists our favorite authors. They are Judy Blume, Roald Dahl, Bruce Coville, Jane Yolen, J. K. Rowling, and Beverly Cleary. We have several events planned for the week. We will have contests, book group meetings, a trip to the public library, an author's visit, and a favorite character party. We are looking forward to the party most of all. We will dress up in costumes, read selections from our favorite books, play games, and serve a buffet featuring appropriate food. So far, the suggested snacks include chocolate turtles, bug juice, fake fried worms (chow mein noodles), and sliced giant peaches.

✗ ERRORS: COMMAS: 14

56 Jarvis and Snappy

Jarvis is a kind, helpful, honest friend. He has short black hair and large, warm, brown eyes. His clothes are clean, stylish, and neat. When I go to Jarvis's house, we play with his dog Snappy. Although his name makes him sound mean, Snappy is actually a gentle, quiet dog. His tail is long, thin, and feathery. He carries it high, like a flag. Snappy's nose is black, wide, cold, and wet. He loves to poke it in my face when I am lying down. His ears are floppy, soft, and silky. They fly out behind him when he runs. Snappy's tongue is pink, rough, and wet. He is always ready to plant a big, sloppy kiss on my cheek. Just like Jarvis, Snappy likes everybody, and everybody likes him.

✗ ERRORS: COMMAS: 17

Name: _____ Date: _____

Children's Book Week   55

Our class is celebrating Children's Book Week. We made a chart. It lists our favorite

authors. They are Judy Blume Roald Dahl Bruce Coville Jane Yolen J. K. Rowling and

Beverly Cleary. We have several events planned for the week. We will have contests

book group meetings a trip to the public library an author's visit and a favorite

character party. We are looking forward to the party most of all. We will dress up in

costumes read selections from our favorite books play games and serve a buffet

featuring appropriate food. So far, the suggested snacks include chocolate turtles bug

juice fake fried worms (chow mein noodles), and sliced giant peaches.

✔ LOOK FOR: ITEMS IN A SERIES

Name: _____ Date: _____

Jarvis and Snappy   56

Jarvis is a kind helpful honest friend. He has short black hair and large warm brown

eyes. His clothes are clean stylish and neat. When I go to Jarvis's house, we play

with his dog Snappy. Although his name makes him sound mean, Snappy is actually

a gentle quiet dog. His tail is long thin and feathery. He carries it high, like a flag.

Snappy's nose is black wide cold and wet. He loves to poke it in my face when I am

lying down. His ears are floppy soft and silky. They fly out behind him when he runs.

Snappy's tongue is pink rough and wet. He is always ready to plant a big sloppy kiss on

my cheek. Just like Jarvis, Snappy likes everybody, and everybody likes him.

✔ LOOK FOR: CONSECUTIVE ADJECTIVES

57 **Puffin Parents**

When it is time for a tufted puffin to lay her eggs, she finds a crevice in a rocky

cliff above the sea, and she makes a depression inside to serve as her nest. In this

protected spot, she lays one white egg. After the egg hatches, both parents feed the

growing chick. The pigeon-sized seabirds fly low over the water, and then they dive

under the surface. They swim quickly, and they gather tiny fish in their beaks. After

feeding the hungry chick, each parent returns to the sea for more fish. It is hard work,

but the devoted puffin parents do not mind. Because they love their little chick, they

are willing to do everything they can to keep it healthy.

ERRORS: COMMAS: 9

58 **A Cure for the Moving Blues**

When Jason's family moved to Union City, he was depressed. Although Union City was

a great town, Jason had lived in Uptonville all of his life, and all of his friends were there.

While movers carried boxes into the new house, Jason sat on the steps and stared across

the street. His little sister came up to him and pulled on his arm, but Jason would not

budge. After the movers left, Jason's father begged him to come upstairs and see his

new room, but Jason sat as still as the stone lions in front of the Uptonville library. Shortly

after his father went into the house, something happened that made Jason very happy. A

boy his own age raced up the sidewalk, and he stopped in front of their house. Because

the boy had been running, it took a minute for him to catch his breath. "I'm Jerry, and I'm

so glad to see you," he said. "We're neighbors, and I hope we'll soon be friends."

ERRORS: COMMAS: 12

Name: _____ Date: _____

Puffin Parents 57 ✓

When it is time for a tufted puffin to lay her eggs she finds a crevice in a rocky cliff above the sea and she makes a depression inside to serve as her nest. In this protected spot she lays one white egg. After the egg hatches both parents feed the growing chick. The pigeon-sized seabirds fly low over the water and then they dive under the surface. They swim quickly and they gather tiny fish in their beaks. After feeding the hungry chick each parent returns to the sea for more fish. It is hard work but the devoted puffin parents do not mind. Because they love their little chick they are willing to do everything they can to keep it healthy.

✔ LOOK FOR: INTRODUCTORY CLAUSES AND INDEPENDENT CLAUSES

Name: _____ Date: _____

A Cure for the Moving Blues 58 ✓

When Jason's family moved to Union City he was depressed. Although Union City was a great town Jason had lived in Uptonville all of his life and all of his friends were there. While movers carried boxes into the new house Jason sat on the steps and stared across the street. His little sister came up to him and pulled on his arm but Jason would not budge. After the movers left Jason's father begged him to come upstairs and see his new room but Jason sat as still as the stone lions in front of the Uptonville library. Shortly after his father went into the house something happened that made Jason very happy. A boy his own age raced up the sidewalk and he stopped in front of their house. Because the boy had been running it took a minute for him to catch his breath. "I'm Jerry and I'm so glad to see you," he said. "We're neighbors and I hope we'll soon be friends."

✔ LOOK FOR: INTRODUCTORY CLAUSES AND INDEPENDENT CLAUSES

60 All About Fish

225 N. Karon Rd.

Clifton, CA 90955

March 12, 2010

Mr. Terrance Wilcox

Wilcox Aquarium Supplies

308 N. Yeats Blvd.

Clifton, CA 90955

Dear Mr. Wilcox:

Thank you for visiting our class. Before your visit, I knew nothing about fish. Now, I understand more. Dad is planning to buy me a small tank, and he will also buy me fish. I have a list of equipment, and I know which kinds of fish are likely to survive. I want a pump, a filter, gravel, food, a light, a tank, and some calico goldfish. Their metallic, pearly scales are pretty. We will visit your shop soon!

Sincerely,

Ryan Hart

ERRORS: COMMAS: 14

59 The Last Ice Age

259 N. Garden Ln.

Kingston, ON K6R 0H7

January 28, 2010

Dr. Peter R. Farnsworth

557 Martin Blvd.

Clancy, ON M7T 0T6

Dear Dr. Farnsworth:

Thank you for answering my questions about the last ice age. I have read several books and some good material on the Internet, but there were still some concepts that I did not understand. Our conversation and the Web sites you suggested helped a lot. I enjoyed learning about moraines, glaciers, cirques, and crevasses. When we visit the Columbia Ice Field next summer, Dad says that he will introduce us. Of course, I look forward to meeting you.

Sincerely,

David McKinsey

ERRORS: COMMAS: 10

Name: _____ Date: _____

59 · The Last Ice Age

259 N. Garden Ln.

Kingston ON K6R 0H7

January 28 2010

Dr. Peter R. Farnsworth

557 Martin Blvd.

Clancy ON M7T 0T6

Dear Dr. Farnsworth:

Thank you for answering my questions about the last ice age. I have read several books and some good material on the Internet but there were still some concepts that I did not understand. Our conversation and the Web sites you suggested helped a lot. I enjoyed learning about moraines glaciers cirques and crevasses. When we visit the Columbia Ice Field next summer Dad says that he will introduce us. Of course I look forward to meeting you.

Sincerely

David McKinsey

Name: _____ Date: _____

60 · All About Fish

225 N. Karon Rd.

Clifton CA 90955

March 12 2010

Mr. Terrance Wilcox

Wilcox Aquarium Supplies

308 N. Yeats Blvd.

Clifton CA 90955

Dear Mr. Wilcox:

Thank you for visiting our class. Before your visit I knew nothing about fish. Now I understand more. Dad is planning to buy me a small tank and he will also buy me fish. I have a list of equipment and I know which kinds of fish are likely to survive. I want a pump, a filter gravel food a light a tank and some calico goldfish. Their metallic pearly scales are pretty. We will visit your shop soon!

Sincerely

Ryan Hart

Studying Instead

To: dan@nomail.zap
From: martin@nomail.zap

Dear Dan,

Thanks for inviting me to the movies. I'd love to come, but I can't. Mom won't let me go out. She's upset because I didn't pass the test last week. I'm not surprised, since I haven't studied much lately. I shouldn't have watched the hockey game on Monday. That wasn't smart. If I could do it over again, I wouldn't make the same choice. Mom's determined to make a change. I wish she'd let me go, but I don't think she will. Here's an idea. If you aren't doing anything tonight, I'm sure she'll let you come over to help me study. Think about it.

Your friend,
Martin

 ERRORS: APOSTROPHES: 17

Science Museum Excursion

To: dennis@nomail.zap
From: anthony@nomail.zap

Dear Dennis,

Have you heard about the exhibit at the science museum? It's opening this weekend. They're inviting an astronaut to speak on Saturday. He's spent time on the International Space Station, and I'd like to meet him. Wouldn't you? David and I are going, and you're welcome to join us. We're leaving at 12:30. I wanted to go earlier, but Dad couldn't miss an appointment. I haven't asked what time we're leaving. It'll probably be 5:00. It shouldn't be any later than 6:00. I'm looking forward to it. I'll be disappointed if you can't come!

Sincerely,
Anthony

ERRORS: APOSTROPHES: 15

66 DAILY EDITING • GRADE 5 • CD-104254 • © CARSON-DELLOSA

Name: _____ Date: _____

Studying Instead 61

To: dan@nomail.zap
From: martin@nomail.zap

Dear Dan,

Thanks for inviting me to the movies. Id love to come, but I cant. Mom wont let me go out. Shes upset because I didnt pass the test last week. Im not surprised, since I havent studied much lately. I shouldnt have watched the hockey game on Monday. That wasnt smart. If I could do it over again, I wouldnt make the same choice. Moms determined to make a change. I wish shed let me go, but I dont think she will. Heres an idea. If you arent doing anything tonight, Im sure shell let you come over to help me study. Think about it.

Your friend,
Martin

LOOK FOR: CONTRACTIONS

Name: _____ Date: _____

Science Museum Excursion 62

To: dennis@nomail.zap
From: anthony@nomail.zap

Dear Dennis,

Have you heard about the exhibit at the science museum? Its opening this weekend. Theyre inviting an astronaut to speak on Saturday. Hes spent time on the International Space Station, and Id like to meet him. Wouldnt you? David and I are going, and youre welcome to join us. Were leaving at 12:30. I wanted to go earlier, but Dad couldnt miss an appointment. I havent asked what time were leaving. Itll probably be 5:00. It shouldnt be any later than 6:00. Im looking forward to it. Ill be disappointed if you cant come!

Sincerely,
Anthony

LOOK FOR: CONTRACTIONS

63 Eduardo's Friends' Hobbies

Eduardo has many interesting friends. Blake's hobby is running model trains. Anthony's stamp collection is the best in town; he has stamps from all over the world. Ben's coin album is almost full, and he even has a few coins from ancient Rome. Dave's two German shepherds keep him busy, especially when he is training them for dog shows. Cole's cartoons look very professional, and he is working on a graphic novel. Andrew's video games teach him about robotics; he wants to be a surgeon like his father. Dustin's sports cards are so valuable that they might pay for his college education. Eduardo is writing an article about all of his friends' hobbies. He is planning to send it to a children's magazine.

✗ ERRORS: APOSTROPHES: 9

64 Pet Pictures

Nick's club made an album with pictures of the members' pets. Each pet's picture was taken by its owner. Luke has two dogs; their names are Lucky and Happy. Lucky's picture is a little bigger than Happy's. Nathan has three hamsters; his hamsters' names are Teeny, Tiny, and Tom. Teeny's picture is the cutest. He was running on a wheel. Gavin has a goldfish; his fish's name is Goldie. Nick's pet is a cat named Whiskers. When Gavin warned Nick to keep the cat's picture away from Goldie's, everybody laughed.

✗ ERRORS: APOSTROPHES: 11

Name: _____ Date: _____

Eduardo's Friends' Hobbies (63)

Eduardo has many interesting friends. Blakes hobby is running model trains. Anthonys stamp collection is the best in town; he has stamps from all over the world. Bens coin album is almost full, and he even has a few coins from ancient Rome. Daves two German shepherds keep him busy, especially when he is training them for dog shows. Coles cartoons look very professional, and he is working on a graphic novel. Andrews video games teach him about robotics; he wants to be a surgeon like his father. Dustins sports cards are so valuable that they might pay for his college education. Eduardo is writing an article about all of his friends hobbies. He is planning to send it to a childrens magazine.

LOOK FOR: SINGULAR AND PLURAL POSSESSIVES

Name: _____ Date: _____

Pet Pictures (64)

Nicks club made an album with pictures of the members pets. Each pets picture was taken by its owner. Luke has two dogs; their names are Lucky and Happy. Luckys picture is a little bigger than Happys. Nathan has three hamsters; his hamsters names are Teeny, Tiny, and Tom. Teenys picture is the cutest. He was running on a wheel. Gavin has a goldfish; his fishs name is Goldie. Nicks pet is a cat named Whiskers. When Gavin warned Nick to keep the cats picture away from Goldies, everybody laughed.

LOOK FOR: SINGULAR AND PLURAL POSSESSIVES

65 Playing Basketball in the Park

To: marcos@nomail.zap
From: juan@nomail.zap

Dear Marcos,

Im planning to meet Kevin at Davids house on Saturday morning. Were walking to the park with Kevins older brother. Hes on Summitville Highs basketball team. Hell help us with our shots. Im hoping to be on that team someday; arent you? Wouldnt you like to come with us? For lunch, well go downtown. Theres a new sandwich shop on Main Street. I havent been there yet, but my brothers friends say its great. Theyre usually right. If you cant make it on Saturday, dont worry. Well probably do the same thing every weekend this spring.

Your friend,
Juan

ERRORS: APOSTROPHES: 19

66 Family Friends

Camilles best friend is Marcella. Theyre in different classes this year, but theyve known each other since preschool. They havent spent more than a few days apart in their lives. Marcellas mom is Camilles fathers boss. Marcellas father is Camilles uncles business partner. The two families friendship has lasted more than 15 years. Marcella has two older brothers, and Camille has one. Theyre in high school now, but theyll be in college soon. The boys relationship is very close. They dont hesitate to call each other for support. Each boys happiness is important to the other two. Camille and Marcella feel the same way about each other.

ERRORS: APOSTROPHES: 16

Name: _____ Date: _____

Playing Basketball in the Park (65)

To: marcos@nomail.zap
From: juan@nomail.zap

Dear Marcos,

Im planning to meet Kevin at Davids house on Saturday morning. Were walking to the park with Kevins older brother. Hes on Summitville Highs basketball team. Hell help us with our shots. Im hoping to be on that team someday; arent you? Wouldnt you like to come with us? For lunch, well go downtown. Theres a new sandwich shop on Main Street. I havent been there yet, but my brothers friends say its great. Theyre usually right. If you cant make it on Saturday, dont worry. Well probably do the same thing every weekend this spring.

Your friend,
Juan

✔ MIXED REVIEW

Name: _____ Date: _____

Family Friends (66)

Camilles best friend is Marcella. Theyre in different classes this year, but theyve known each other since preschool. They havent spent more than a few days apart in their lives. Marcellas mom is Camilles fathers boss. Marcellas father is Camilles uncles business partner. The two families friendship has lasted more than 15 years. Marcella has two older brothers, and Camille has one. Theyre in high school now, but theyll be in college soon. The boys relationship is very close. They dont hesitate to call each other for support. Each boys happiness is important to the other two. Camille and Marcella feel the same way about each other.

✔ MIXED REVIEW

67 Part of the Team

Tony spotted Robert on the other side of the playground. "Robert!" he called. "Wait!"

Robert waved, and Tony hurried to meet him. "Have you heard from Coach Morris yet?"

"No, not yet," Robert said.

"I haven't heard anything either," Tony said.

"It's only been a week though," Robert said.

"You're right," Tony agreed. "I'm sure he'll call soon."

"I hope so," Robert said. "I really want to be on that team!"

 ERRORS: QUOTATION MARKS: 18

68 A Rainy Day

Laura and Anna were sitting in Anna's room watching the rain. "I hope it stops," Laura said.

"I do too," Anna said. "I'm tired of staying inside."

"What should we play?" Laura asked.

"What games do you have?" Anna asked.

"We could put together a jigsaw puzzle," Laura suggested.

"How many pieces?" Anna asked.

"One thousand," Laura said.

Anna laughed. "That would take all week," she said.

"I know," Laura said. Then, she opened her closet door and reached for something on a

shelf. She took down a checkerboard and a wooden box. "This is always fun," she said.

ERRORS: QUOTATION MARKS: 19

Name: _____ Date: _____

Part of the Team 67

Tony spotted Robert on the other side of the playground. "Robert!" he called. Wait!

Robert waved, and Tony hurried to meet him. Have you heard from Coach Morris yet?

No, not yet, Robert said.

I haven't heard anything either, Tony said.

It's only been a week though, Robert said.

You're right, Tony agreed. I'm sure he'll call soon.

I hope so, Robert said. I really want to be on that team!

✔ LOOK FOR: DIALOGUE

Name: _____ Date: _____

A Rainy Day 68

Laura and Anna were sitting in Anna's room watching the rain. "I hope it stops, Laura said.

I do too, Anna said. I'm tired of staying inside.

What should we play? Laura asked.

What games do you have? Anna asked.

We could put together a jigsaw puzzle," Laura suggested.

How many pieces? Anna asked.

One thousand, Laura said.

Anna laughed. That would take all week, she said.

I know, Laura said. Then, she opened her closet door and reached for something on a

shelf. She took down a checkerboard and a wooden box. This is always fun," she said.

✔ LOOK FOR: DIALOGUE

69 Measurement Math

Andrew was the leader of the math group. "First, we must decide what to measure," he said.

"I would like to measure the length of a lunch table," Stephanie said.

"OK, write that down," Andrew said. He handed her a sheet of paper. "Do not forget to write your name," he added.

Next, Marcos raised his hand. "I will measure the distance to the office," he said.

"Add that to the list," Andrew said.

"Madison and I will measure the length of the library," Kathleen said.

"Good," Andrew said. "I will measure the length of the front walkway."

ERRORS: QUOTATION MARKS: 13; COMMAS: 5

70 A Break from School

Mrs. Anderson was sweeping her front porch when Carlos walked up the street.

"Good morning, Carlos," she said.

"Good morning, Mrs. Anderson," Carlos said.

"You're home early," Mrs. Anderson said.

"Yes, it's conference day at school," Carlos said.

"You're lucky," Mrs. Anderson said.

"Yes, I know," Carlos said.

"I'm sure you have something special planned," Mrs. Anderson said.

"Yes, my friend is meeting me in a few minutes," Carlos said. "We're going to the hobby shop."

"Have a good time," Mrs. Anderson said.

ERRORS: QUOTATION MARKS: 10; COMMAS: 7

Name: _____ Date: _____

Measurement Math 69

Andrew was the leader of the math group. First, we must decide what to measure"

he said.

I would like to measure the length of a lunch table, Stephanie said.

OK, write that down" Andrew said. He handed her a sheet of paper. Do not forget to

write your name, he added.

Next, Marcos raised his hand. I will measure the distance to the office, he said.

Add that to the list" Andrew said.

Madison and I will measure the length of the library" Kathleen said.

Good" Andrew said. I will measure the length of the front walkway.

✔ LOOK FOR: DIALOGUE

Name: _____ Date: _____

A Break from School 70

Mrs. Anderson was sweeping her front porch when Carlos walked up the street.

"Good morning, Carlos" she said.

Good morning, Mrs. Anderson" Carlos said.

You're home early, Mrs. Anderson said.

"Yes, it's conference day at school" Carlos said.

"You're lucky, Mrs. Anderson said.

Yes, I know" Carlos said.

I'm sure you have something special planned" Mrs. Anderson said.

Yes, my friend is meeting me in a few minutes" Carlos said. We're going to the hobby shop.

Have a good time" Mrs. Anderson said.

✔ LOOK FOR: DIALOGUE

71 — Geography Project

Leslie, Kimberley, and Janelle were working together on a world geography project.

"Do you have the atlas?" Janelle asked.

"Yes, here it is," Kimberly said, handing her the book.

"What are you looking for?" Leslie asked.

"The longest river in South America," Janelle said.

"That's easy!" exclaimed Kimberly. She grinned mischievously.

"What is it?" Janelle demanded.

Kimberley opened the atlas to the correct page and pointed.

"The Amazon!" Janelle exclaimed.

X ERRORS: QUOTATION MARKS: 9; QUESTION MARKS: 3; EXCLAMATION POINTS: 2

---

72 — King Is Missing!

Jimmy spotted Gavin in the driveway.

"What are you doing?" Jimmy called.

"My dog King is missing," Gavin called back.

"Oh no!" Jimmy exclaimed. He hurried to help his friend.

"Did you see him in front of your house?" Gavin asked.

"No, I'm sorry," Jimmy said.

"I've looked all over the yard, and I can't find him," Gavin said.

Just then, Jimmy heard something. "Listen!" he exclaimed.

A dog barked. King had been in the house the whole time!

X ERRORS: QUOTATION MARKS: 10; QUESTION MARKS: 2; EXCLAMATION POINTS: 2

Name: _____   Date: _____

Geography Project 71 ✓

Leslie, Kimberley, and Janelle were working together on a world geography project.

Do you have the atlas," Janelle asked.

Yes, here it is, Kimberly said, handing her the book.

What are you looking for," Leslie asked.

The longest river in South America, Janelle said.

That's easy," exclaimed Kimberly. She grinned mischievously.

What is it," Janelle demanded.

Kimberley opened the atlas to the correct page and pointed.

The Amazon," Janelle exclaimed.

✓ **LOOK FOR: DIALOGUE**

Name: _____   Date: _____

King Is Missing! 72 ✓

Jimmy spotted Gavin in the driveway.

What are you doing," Jimmy called.

My dog King is missing, Gavin called back.

Oh no," Jimmy exclaimed. He hurried to help his friend.

Did you see him in front of your house," Gavin asked.

No, I'm sorry, Jimmy said.

I've looked all over the yard, and I can't find him, Gavin said.

Just then, Jimmy heard something. Listen," he exclaimed.

A dog barked. King had been in the house the whole time!

✓ **LOOK FOR: DIALOGUE**

73 Language Arts Festival

Next week, our school will hold its annual Language Arts Festival. Krista and I will recite "The Lobster Quadrille" by Lewis Carroll. She will say, "Will you walk a little faster?" Then, I will say, "Said the whiting to a snail." After we finish that wonderfully silly poem, Krista will introduce the next performers. She will say, "Mrs. Gordon's class has a special treat for you." Then, the third graders will sing "If You're Happy and You Know It." Other groups will recite "Mice" by Rose Fyleman and "Splinter" by Carl Sandburg. The second graders will perform a play based on the story "Hansel and Gretel." The announcement on our school's Web site says it all. It reads, "Don't miss the best program of the year!"

ERRORS: QUOTATION MARKS: 18

74 Tyler's Tongue Twisters

My little brother Tyler loves tongue twisters. He recited "Peter Piper" every day last week. He marched around the living room repeating, "Peter Piper picked a peck of pickled peppers," while Mom was trying to read "Cinderella" to my little sister. Finally, Mom told him to go outside. This week he is saying, "How much wood would a woodchuck chuck?" He also knows "Shy Sarah," "A Big Black Bug," "Betty Botter's Butter," and "Fuzzy Wuzzy Was a Bear." Yesterday, I stumped Tyler. When our dog Shane spread trash all over the kitchen, I said, "Shame, Shane, shame!" Tyler is still trying to repeat that tongue-twisting phrase.

ERRORS: QUOTATION MARKS: 14

Name: _____ Date: _____

Language Arts Festival 73 ✓

Next week, our school will hold its annual Language Arts Festival. Krista and I will recite The Lobster Quadrille by Lewis Carroll. She will say, Will you walk a little faster? Then, I will say, Said the whiting to a snail. After we finish that wonderfully silly poem, Krista will introduce the next performers. She will say, Mrs. Gordon's class has a special treat for you. Then, the third graders will sing If You're Happy and You Know It. Other groups will recite Mice by Rose Fyleman and Splinter by Carl Sandburg. The second graders will perform a play based on the story Hansel and Gretel. The announcement on our school's Web site says it all. It reads, Don't miss the best program of the year!

✓ LOOK FOR: SONG, STORY, & POEM TITLES AND QUOTED MATERIAL

Name: _____ Date: _____

Tyler's Tongue Twisters 74 ✓

My little brother Tyler loves tongue twisters. He recited Peter Piper every day last week. He marched around the living room repeating, Peter Piper picked a peck of pickled peppers, while Mom was trying to read Cinderella to my little sister. Finally, Mom told him to go outside. This week he is saying, How much wood would a woodchuck chuck? He also knows Shy Sarah," A Big Black Bug, "Betty Botter's Butter, and Fuzzy Wuzzy Was a Bear. Yesterday, I stumped Tyler. When our dog Shane spread trash all over the kitchen, I said, "Shame, Shane, shame!" Tyler is still trying to repeat that tongue-twisting phrase.

✓ LOOK FOR: STORY AND TONGUE TWISTER TITLES

75 Common Word Roots

Word roots can help you understand longer words. The word *photography* comes from two common roots. The word root *photo* means "light." The word root *graph* means "writing." In a camera, light writes on the film or sensor to record the picture. The word *autograph* also comes from the word root *graph*. The root *auto* means "self." When you sign an autograph for someone, you write it yourself. Early recordings were made on vinyl disks called *phonograph records*. The word root *phone* means "sound," so the word *phonograph* means "sound writing." Can you think of other words that contain these common roots?

✗ ERRORS: QUOTATION MARKS: 10

76 Scientific Word Roots

The names of many sciences end with the word root *logy*. It means "the study or theory of something." The word root *bio* means "life," so the word *biology* means "the study of living things." The word root *geo* means "Earth," so the word *geology* means "the study of Earth." The word root *cardio* means "heart," so *cardiology* means "the study of the heart." The word root *psych* means "mind or soul," so the science of *psychology* studies human thoughts and emotions. As you can see, if you understand word roots, it is easier to learn scientific terms.

✗ ERRORS: QUOTATION MARKS: 16

Name: _____   Date: _____

Common Word Roots   75

Word roots can help you understand longer words. The word *photography* comes from two common roots. The word root *photo* means light. The word root *graph* means writing. In a camera, light writes on the film or sensor to record the picture. The word *autograph* also comes from the word root *graph*. The root *auto* means self. When you sign an autograph for someone, you write it yourself. Early recordings were made on vinyl disks called *phonograph records*. The word root *phone* means sound, so the word *phonograph* means sound writing. Can you think of other words that contain these common roots?

✔ LOOK FOR: DEFINITIONS

Name: _____   Date: _____

Scientific Word Roots   76

The names of many sciences end with the word root *logy*. It means the study or theory of something. The word root *bio* means life, so the word *biology* means the study of living things. The word root *geo* means Earth, so the word *geology* means the study of Earth. The word root *cardio* means heart, so *cardiology* means the study of the heart. The word root *psych* means mind or soul, so the science of *psychology* studies human thoughts and emotions. As you can see, if you understand word roots, it is easier to learn scientific terms.

✔ LOOK FOR: DEFINITIONS

77 Pourquoi Tales

"Ryan, it is time to present your report," said Mr. Norman as he looked at the schedule on his desk.

Ryan stood up, picked up his papers, and walked to the front of the classroom. He wrote the name of a folktale on the board. It was "How the Tortoise Got Its Shell." He said it was a special kind of story called a *pourquoi tale*. He explained that the name comes from the French word that means "why." He told us the story, and then he listed other pourquoi tales. They included "The Fox and the Fry Bread," "How the Fawn Got Its Spots," "Why Snails Have Shells," and "The Elephant Child."

Then, Ryan surprised us. He told everyone to take out a sheet of paper and a pencil. "It is time for you to write a pourquoi tale of your own!" he exclaimed excitedly.

ERRORS: QUOTATION MARKS: 13; COMMAS: 1; EXCLAMATION POINTS: 1

78 Our Special Spring Program

Holly Street School will hold a spring program next month. Our contribution will be a play based on a special ancient Greek story called a *myth*. The title of the story is "Pandora." I will be the announcer for our class. I will say, "Mrs. Forrest's fifth-grade class is proud to present a famous story about a young woman who was too curious." Next, Mr. Graham's class will recite three poems. They are "What Do We Plant?" by Henry Abbey, "The Cloud" by Percy Bysshe Shelley, and "Daffodils" by William Wordsworth. Ms. Carroll's class will sing "The Ash Grove." At the end of the show, I will ask, "Are you ready for a special surprise?" Then, we will all go to the front of the school where we will plant a tree.

ERRORS: QUOTATION MARKS: 13; QUESTION MARKS: 1

Name: _____ Date: _____

Pourquoi Tales 77

Ryan, it is time to present your report" said Mr. Norman as he looked at the schedule

on his desk.

Ryan stood up, picked up his papers, and walked to the front of the classroom. He

wrote the name of a folktale on the board. It was How the Tortoise Got Its Shell. He said

it was a special kind of story called a *pourquoi tale*. He explained that the name comes

from the French word that means why. He told us the story, and then he listed other

pourquoi tales. They included The Fox and the Fry Bread, "How the Fawn Got Its Spots,

Why Snails Have Shells, and The Elephant Child.

Then, Ryan surprised us. He told everyone to take out a sheet of paper and a pencil.

It is time for you to write a pourquoi tale of your own," he exclaimed excitedly.

✓ MIXED REVIEW

Name: _____ Date: _____

Our Special Spring Program 78

Holly Street School will hold a spring program next month. Our contribution will be

a play based on a special ancient Greek story called a *myth*. The title of the story is

Pandora. I will be the announcer for our class. I will say, Mrs. Forrest's fifth-grade class

is proud to present a famous story about a young woman who was too curious. Next,

Mr. Graham's class will recite three poems. They are What Do We Plant? by Henry

Abbey, The Cloud by Percy Bysshe Shelley, and Daffodils by William Wordsworth.

Ms. Carroll's class will sing The Ash Grove. At the end of the show, I will ask, Are you

ready for a special surprise," Then, we will all go to the front of the school where we

will plant a tree.

✓ MIXED REVIEW

Books and Movies for Fifth Graders

Our school library has a shelf that features books for fifth graders. This month's selections include <u>Hoot</u> by Carl Hiaasen, <u>Sign of the Beaver</u> by Elizabeth George Speare, <u>Stepping on the Cracks</u> by Mary Hahn Downing, <u>Beyond the Divide</u> by Kathryn Lasky, <u>Kokopelli's Flute</u> by Will Hobbs, <u>Number the Stars</u> by Lois Lowry, <u>Woodsong</u> by Gary Paulsen, <u>The Birchbark House</u> by Louise Erdrich, and <u>Going Through the Gate</u> by Janet S. Anderson. The public library recommends films for fifth graders too. So far, I have seen <u>The Chronicles of Narnia: The Lion, the Witch and the Wardrobe</u>, <u>Lemony Snicket's A Series of Unfortunate Events</u>, <u>The March of the Penguins</u>, and <u>Harry Potter and the Chamber of Secrets</u>. I loved them all!

✗ ERRORS: UNDERLINES: 13

 Film and Book Adventures

Many books have been made into movies. I often read a book first and then rent the film at our local video store. This year, I have seen <u>Alice in Wonderland</u>, <u>The Wizard of Oz</u>, <u>My Side of the Mountain</u>, <u>The Incredible Journey</u>, <u>The Black Stallion</u>, <u>Bridge to Terabithia</u>, <u>Charlotte's Web</u>, <u>Harry Potter and the Sorcerer's Stone</u>, and <u>The Hobbit</u>. Sometimes, I like to read books without seeing the story on-screen. It is fun to picture the characters and events in my mind. Recently, I have enjoyed <u>Everywhere</u> by Bruce Brooks, <u>The Pinballs</u> by Betsy Byars, <u>The Barn</u> by Avi, <u>I Am the Cheese</u> by Robert Cormier, <u>Dateline: Troy</u> by Paul Fleischman, and <u>Nightfather</u> by Carl Friedman.

✗ ERRORS: UNDERLINES: 15

Name: _____   Date: _____

Books and Movies for Fifth Graders 79

Our school library has a shelf that features books for fifth graders. This month's selections include Hoot by Carl Hiaasen, Sign of the Beaver by Elizabeth George Speare, Stepping on the Cracks by Mary Hahn Downing, Beyond the Divide by Kathryn Lasky, Kokopelli's Flute by Will Hobbs, Number the Stars by Lois Lowry, Woodsong by Gary Paulsen, The Birchbark House by Louise Erdrich, and Going Through the Gate by Janet S. Anderson. The public library recommends films for fifth graders too. So far, I have seen The Chronicles of Narnia: The Lion, the Witch and the Wardrobe, Lemony Snicket's A Series of Unfortunate Events, The March of the Penguins, and Harry Potter and the Chamber of Secrets. I loved them all!

✔ LOOK FOR: BOOK AND MOVIE TITLES

Name: _____   Date: _____

Film and Book Adventures 80

Many books have been made into movies. I often read a book first and then rent the film at our local video store. This year, I have seen Alice in Wonderland, The Wizard of Oz, My Side of the Mountain, The Incredible Journey, The Black Stallion, Bridge to Terabithia, Charlotte's Web, Harry Potter and the Sorcerer's Stone, and The Hobbit. Sometimes, I like to read books without seeing the story on-screen. It is fun to picture the characters and events in my mind. Recently, I have enjoyed Everywhere by Bruce Brooks, The Pinballs by Betsy Byars, The Barn by Avi, I Am the Cheese by Robert Cormier, Dateline: Troy by Paul Fleischman, and Nightfather by Carl Friedman.

✔ LOOK FOR: BOOK AND MOVIE TITLES

81 Systems in the Human Body

Our bodies have many systems(sets of organs) that work together. The nervous system (the brain and the nerves) is in charge. It sends, processes, and receives messages. It is like a computer using the Internet. The circulatory system(the heart, the arteries, and the veins) and the respiratory system(the trachea, the bronchial tubes, and the lungs) work together to deliver supplies to the cells. The skeletal system(the skull and other bones) and the muscular system(the muscles and tendons) work together to help us stand and move. The esophagus, the stomach, the liver, and the intestines(the digestive system) deliver needed food supplies to our cells.

ERRORS: PARENTHESES: 14

82 The Five Senses

In the human body, each sense organ sends special information to the brain. The ears control the sense of hearing(audition). The nose controls the sense of smell (olfaction) The skin controls the sense of touch(tactition). The tongue controls the sense of taste (gustation) Finally, the eyes control the sense of sight(vision) Our senses keep us in touch with the world around us. Some people do not have the use of one or more senses. Helen Keller(a famous author and lecturer) could neither see nor hear. She used the senses of touch, taste, and smell to learn about her world.

ERRORS: PARENTHESES: 9

Name: _____ Date: _____

Systems in the Human Body (81) ✓

Our bodies have many systems sets of organs that work together. The nervous system the brain and the nerves is in charge. It sends, processes, and receives messages. It is like a computer using the Internet. The circulatory system the heart, the arteries, and the veins and the respiratory system the trachea, the bronchial tubes, and the lungs work together to deliver supplies to the cells. The skeletal system the skull and other bones and the muscular system the muscles and tendons work together to help us stand and move. The esophagus, the stomach, the liver, and the intestines the digestive system deliver needed food supplies to our cells.

✔ LOOK FOR: PARENTHETICAL WORDS, PHRASES, AND DEFINITIONS

Name: _____ Date: _____

The Five Senses (82) ✓

In the human body, each sense organ sends special information to the brain. The ears control the sense of hearing audition). The nose controls the sense of smell (olfaction. The skin controls the sense of touch tactition. The tongue controls the sense of taste (gustation. Finally, the eyes control the sense of sight vision. Our senses keep us in touch with the world around us. Some people do not have the use of one or more senses. Helen Keller a famous author and lecturer could neither see nor hear. She used the senses of touch, taste, and smell to learn about her world.

✔ LOOK FOR: PARENTHETICAL WORDS, PHRASES, AND DEFINITIONS

83 Woeful Woofer Part I

Woofer, that silly old dog of ours, is home again. This is how the whole crazy drama

started. I called—actually, whistled, for Woofer to come to dinner. Usually, he dashes

into the kitchen right away. The house was quiet, absolutely still. I felt a pang of worry

and panic. Woofer's bad habits, chewing up books and tracking mud into the house,

upset everyone in the family. There was only one reason to keep that dog, we loved

him. The thought of losing him, even for a short time, was unbearable. I have to go now,

it's time for dinner. I will finish the story tomorrow.

ERRORS: DASHES: 10

84 Woeful Woofer Part II

This is what happened next. I was searching desperately for Woofer. Carol, my older

sister, finally came home from school. I told her that Woofer was missing and that

he was possibly lost or hurt. She helped me look in every room, even under the beds.

We could not find Woofer anywhere. Carol hurried to tell our neighbors. They all love

Woofer too. Mr. Marcus, Maggie's dad, jumped into his car. Mrs. Linden, the retired

teacher next door, walked around the block calling, "Woofer! Woofer!" Finally,

Nicholas, Carol's boyfriend, walked up the street. Behind him trotted our dog. Woofer,

always ready for a walk, had met him in front of the house and followed him to the

corner store.

ERRORS: DASHES: 11

Name: _____ Date: _____

Woeful Woofer Part I ⑧③

Woofer that silly old dog of ours is home again. This is how the whole crazy drama started. I called—actually, whistled for Woofer to come to dinner. Usually, he dashes into the kitchen right away. The house was quiet absolutely still. I felt a pang of worry and panic. Woofer's bad habits chewing up books and tracking mud into the house upset everyone in the family. There was only one reason to keep that dog we loved him. The thought of losing him even for a short time was unbearable. I have to go now it's time for dinner. I will finish the story tomorrow.

✔ LOOK FOR: SUDDEN BREAKS OR INTERRUPTIONS

Name: _____ Date: _____

Woeful Woofer Part II ⑧④

This is what happened next. I was searching desperately for Woofer. Carol my older sister finally came home from school. I told her that Woofer was missing and that he was possibly lost or hurt. She helped me look in every room even under the beds. We could not find Woofer anywhere. Carol hurried to tell our neighbors. They all love Woofer too. Mr. Marcus Maggie's dad jumped into his car. Mrs. Linden the retired teacher next door walked around the block calling, "Woofer! Woofer!" Finally, Nicholas Carol's boyfriend walked up the street. Behind him trotted our dog. Woofer always ready for a walk had met him in front of the house and followed him to the corner store.

✔ LOOK FOR: SUDDEN BREAKS OR INTERRUPTIONS

Weekend Fun

To: gary@nomail.zap
From: richard@nomail.zap

Dear Gary,

Hey, what did you do this weekend? John called early Saturday morning. He asked, "Would you like to rent some movies?" I looked out the window, and it was raining. "Sure," I said. John's mom picked me up at 10:00 A.M. She drove us to the video store. One-fourth of our favorite films were out. We rented <u>Harry Potter and the Goblet of Fire</u>, <u>Babe</u>, and <u>George of the Jungle</u>. We spent the day eating yummy, buttery popcorn and watching films.

Your friend,
Richard

> ✗ ERRORS: PERIODS: 1; COLONS: 1; HYPHENS: 1; COMMAS: 7; APOSTROPHES: 1; QUOTATION MARKS: 2; QUESTION MARKS: 1; UNDERLINES: 3

 School Newspaper Survey

Our school newspaper (the <u>Bobcat Times</u>) took a survey last week. The results were published today. The first survey question was, "What's your favorite movie?" Two-fifths of the students preferred—big surprise—<u>March of the Penguins</u>. The girls' favorite film was <u>The Princess Diaries</u>; the boys' favorite was <u>Harry Potter and the Sorcerer's Stone</u>. The second survey question was, "What's your favorite poem?" The fifth-grade students' favorites were the following: "Toothpaste" by Michael Rosen, "The Honey Pot" by Alan Riddell, and "Mean Song" by Eve Merriam.

> ✗ ERRORS: SEMICOLONS: 1; COLONS: 1; HYPHENS: 2; COMMAS: 2; APOSTROPHES: 3; QUOTATION MARKS: 4; QUESTION MARKS: 1; UNDERLINES: 3; PARENTHESES: 1; DASHES: 1

Name: _____   Date: _____

Weekend Fun   85

To: gary@nomail.zap
From: richard@nomail.zap

Dear Gary,

Hey what did you do this weekend? John called early Saturday morning He asked, Would you like to rent some movies." I looked out the window and it was raining. Sure" I said. Johns mom picked me up at 1000 A.M. She drove us to the video store. One fourth of our favorite films were out. We rented Harry Potter and the Goblet of Fire Babe and George of the Jungle. We spent the day eating yummy buttery popcorn and watching films.

Your friend
Richard

✔ CUMULATIVE REVIEW

Name: _____   Date: _____

School Newspaper Survey   86

Our school newspaper (the Bobcat Times took a survey last week. The results were published today. The first survey question was, "What's your favorite movie." Two fifths of the students preferred big surprise—March of the Penguins. The girls favorite film was The Princess Diaries the boys favorite was Harry Potter and the Sorcerer's Stone. The second survey question was, Whats your favorite poem?" The fifth grade students' favorites were the following Toothpaste by Michael Rosen "The Honey Pot" by Alan Riddell and Mean Song" by Eve Merriam.

✔ CUMULATIVE REVIEW

87

Agricultural Products

The word *agriculture* comes from two old Roman words that mean "field" and

"cultivation." Agricultural ~~product~~ [products] include field ~~crop~~ [crops], such as ~~oat~~ [oats], ~~vegetable~~ [vegetables],

and cotton. Orchard crops, such as ~~apple~~ [apples], ~~orange~~ [oranges], and ~~nut~~ [nuts], are important ~~source~~ [sources]

of income for ~~farmer~~ [farmers] in ~~part~~ [parts] of the world where the climate is mild. Fruits grown on

vines, such as berries and ~~grape~~ [grapes], are also important. Many farmers and ~~rancher~~ [ranchers] raise

livestock. ~~Cow~~ [Cows] and ~~goat~~ [goats] are raised to provide people with meat and milk. ~~Chicken~~ [Chickens] are

raised for meat, ~~egg~~ [eggs], and ~~feather~~ [feathers].

⊗ ERRORS: REGULAR PLURALS: 17

88

Leather

Animal ~~skin~~ [skins] or *hides* have been used for centuries. Tanned animal ~~skin~~ [skins] are known as

leather. Because leather is strong and flexible, it is used to make ~~belt~~ [belts], shoes, ~~purse~~ [purses],

hats, and ~~coat~~ [coats]. ~~Cowboy~~ [Cowboys] wear leather ~~boot~~ [boots] and ~~chap~~ [chaps]. ~~Saddle~~ [Saddles] are made of leather.

Motorcycle ~~rider~~ [riders] wear leather ~~pant~~ [pants] and ~~jacket~~ [jackets] to protect their ~~leg~~ [legs] and ~~arm~~ [arms]. Leather is

also used to make ~~baseball~~ [baseballs], ~~basketball~~ [basketballs], and ~~football~~ [footballs]. In North America, most leather

is made from cattle hides. Skins from deer, ~~pig~~ [pigs], goats, and sheep are used to make

special ~~kind~~ [kinds] of leather.

⊗ ERRORS: REGULAR PLURALS: 19

Name: _____ Date: _____

Agricultural Products (87)

The word *agriculture* comes from two old Roman words that mean "field" and
"cultivation." Agricultural product include field crop, such as oat, vegetable,
and cotton. Orchard crops, such as apple, orange, and nut, are important source
of income for farmer in part of the world where the climate is mild. Fruits grown on
vines, such as berries and grape, are also important. Many farmers and rancher raise
livestock. Cow and goat are raised to provide people with meat and milk. Chicken are
raised for meat, egg, and feather.

✔ LOOK FOR: REGULAR PLURALS

Name: _____ Date: _____

Leather (88)

Animal skin or *hides* have been used for centuries. Tanned animal skin are known as
leather. Because leather is strong and flexible, it is used to make belt, shoes, purse,
hats, and coat. Cowboy wear leather boot and chap. Saddle are made of leather.
Motorcycle rider wear leather pant and jacket to protect their leg and arm. Leather is
also used to make baseball, basketball, and football. In North America, most leather
is made from cattle hides. Skins from deer, pig, goats, and sheep are used to make
special kind of leather.

✔ LOOK FOR: REGULAR PLURALS

(89) Weekend at the Farm

I spent the weekend at my grandparents' farm. In the morning, I went to the lake with
my grandfather. On the way, we saw some ~~deers~~ [deer], two ~~mooses~~ [moose], and a pair of ~~wolfs~~ [wolves]. We
also saw a herd of cows with three newborn ~~calfs~~ [calves]. At the lake, Grandpa caught three
types of fish. He caught one catfish, one bass, and one trout. Several other ~~persons~~ [people]
were there. I counted three ~~mans~~ [men], two ~~womans~~ [women], and two ~~childs~~ [children]. We drove back to
the house for lunch. Grandma served roasted chicken, diced ~~tomatos~~ [tomatoes], and mashed
~~potatos~~ [potatoes]. After we ate, I helped my cousin wash the dishes and put them away. He put
the plates on the ~~shelfs~~ [shelves], and I put the spoons, forks, and ~~knifes~~ [knives] in the silverware drawer.
I like the ~~lifes~~ [lives] that my grandparents have at the farm.

ERRORS: IRREGULAR PLURALS: 13

(90) Herding Sheep

Last autumn, our class went to a sheepdog trial. In this event, herding dogs compete
to move sheep around fields and into enclosed areas. Two buses met us in front of the
school. Two teachers, along with their ~~wifes~~ [wives] and ~~childs~~ [children], came with us. The drive was
beautiful. It was autumn; the leaves were red and gold. We saw ~~oxes~~ [oxen], ~~deers~~ [deer], ~~mooses~~ [moose],
and wild ~~gooses~~ [geese] on the way. We also saw some ~~mans~~ [men] and ~~womans~~ [women] camped on the
shore of Lake Myers. The trial was held on a big ranch. Before the trial, we watched
several ~~mouses~~ [mice] scurrying by the barn. They were eating cheese like ~~thiefs~~ [thieves]. The ~~sheeps~~ [sheep]
were in pens. At the beginning of each event, they were released into a field. The
dogs dashed out to herd the ~~sheeps~~ [sheep] into an enclosure. All of us jumped to our ~~foots~~ [feet] to
applaud the dogs' skill.

ERRORS: IRREGULAR PLURALS: 13

Name: _____ Date: _____

Weekend at the Farm (89)

I spent the weekend at my grandparents' farm. In the morning, I went to the lake with my grandfather. On the way, we saw some deers, two mooses, and a pair of wolfs. We also saw a herd of cows with three newborn calfs. At the lake, Grandpa caught three types of fish. He caught one catfish, one bass, and one trout. Several other persons were there. I counted three mans, two womans, and two childs. We drove back to the house for lunch. Grandma served roasted chicken, diced tomatos, and mashed potatos. After we ate, I helped my cousin wash the dishes and put them away. He put the plates on the shelfs, and I put the spoons, forks, and knifes in the silverware drawer. I like the lifes that my grandparents have at the farm.

✔ LOOK FOR: IRREGULAR PLURALS

Name: _____ Date: _____

Herding Sheep (90)

Last autumn, our class went to a sheepdog trial. In this event, herding dogs compete to move sheep around fields and into enclosed areas. Two buses met us in front of the school. Two teachers, along with their wifes and childs, came with us. The drive was beautiful. It was autumn; the leaves were red and gold. We saw oxes, deers, mooses, and wild gooses on the way. We also saw some mans and womans camped on the shore of Lake Myers. The trial was held on a big ranch. Before the trial, we watched several mouses scurrying by the barn. They were eating cheese like thiefs. The sheeps were in pens. At the beginning of each event, they were released into a field. The dogs dashed out to herd the sheeps into an enclosure. All of us jumped to our foots to applaud the dogs' skill.

✔ LOOK FOR: IRREGULAR PLURALS

91   Vacation with Aunt Geneva

April 8, 2010

Dear Journal,

Today, Mom let me use ~~sum~~ [some] of her best ~~stationary~~ [stationery]. I chose a card with ~~reel~~ [real] pressed ~~flour~~ [flower] ~~pedals~~ [petals] on the front. I also borrowed Mom's black gel ~~pin~~ [pen]. I needed the card and the ~~pin~~ [pen] to ~~right~~ [write] a note. I wanted ~~two~~ [to] thank ~~Ant~~ [Aunt] Geneva ~~fore~~ [for] letting me stay with her at Lamar

Manor, a resort hotel on Lake Mariah. I will never forget that ~~weak~~ [week]. The ~~whether~~ [weather] was

perfect. On the first day, I ~~road~~ [rode] a ~~hoarse~~ [horse]. The next day, Aunt Geneva rented a ~~petal~~ [pedal] car,

and we explored a bike ~~root~~ [route] near the golf ~~coarse~~ [course]. What a ~~grate~~ [great] vacation! Best of all,

Aunt Geneva and I had a chance to learn more about each other.

✗   ERRORS: HOMOPHONES: 19

---

92   Home Sick

Last week, I stayed home because I had a fever and a ~~soar~~ [sore] throat. Today, I am

feeling much better, but I am still ~~week~~ [weak] and a little ~~horse~~ [hoarse]. Mom wrote me a note.

At ~~hour~~ [our] school, you must ~~sea~~ [see] the nurse if you are absent ~~four~~ [for] more than ~~too~~ [two]

days. I arrived earlier than usual this morning ~~sew~~ [so] that I ~~wood~~ [would] not have to ~~weight~~ [wait].

Unfortunately, the nurse was late. I sat in a hard ~~blew~~ [blue] chair for more than an ~~our~~ [hour].

~~Their~~ [There] was ~~won~~ [one] good thing about spending extra time in the office. I completed all of

the homework I had ~~mist~~ [missed]! When the nurse arrived, she explained that she had been

caught in a traffic jam. She ~~red~~ [read] my Mom's note and checked my temperature. Then,

she ~~scent~~ [sent] me ~~strait~~ [straight] to class.

✗   ERRORS: HOMOPHONES: 18

Name: _____ Date: _____

Vacation with Aunt Geneva   91

April 8, 2010

Dear Journal,

Today, Mom let me use sum of her best stationary. I chose a card with reel pressed flour pedals on the front. I also borrowed Mom's black gel pin. I needed the card and the pin to right a note. I wanted two thank Ant Geneva fore letting me stay with her at Lamar Manor, a resort hotel on Lake Mariah. I will never forget that weak. The whether was perfect. On the first day, I road a hoarse. The next day, Aunt Geneva rented a petal car, and we explored a bike root near the golf coarse. What a grate vacation! Best of all, Aunt Geneva and I had a chance to learn more about each other.

✔ LOOK FOR: HOMOPHONES

Name: _____ Date: _____

Home Sick   92

Last week, I stayed home because I had a fever and a soar throat. Today, I am feeling much better, but I am still week and a little horse. Mom wrote me a note. At hour school, you must sea the nurse if you are absent four more than too days. I arrived earlier than usual this morning sew that I wood not have to weight. Unfortunately, the nurse was late. I sat in a hard blew chair for more than an our. Their was won good thing about spending extra time in the office. I completed all of the homework I had mist! When the nurse arrived, she explained that she had been caught in a traffic jam. She red my Mom's note and checked my temperature. Then, she scent me strait to class.

✔ LOOK FOR: HOMOPHONES

93 Living History Farm

Today, ~~hour~~ [our] class visited a living history farm. Many other ~~class~~ [classes] were there, ~~sow~~ [so] the

parking lot was full of school buses. First, we visited the pond. Some ducks and ~~gooses~~ [geese]

waddled over to us on their flat, webbed ~~foots~~ [feet]. They wanted food, but we did not have

any. Two ~~womans~~ [women] met us at the museum building. They were wearing clothes from the

pioneer period. They said that they were dressed as farm ~~wifes~~ [wives]. They explained that ~~woo~~ [we]

~~wood~~ [would] soon learn about the ~~lifes~~ [lives] of early farm ~~family~~ [families] in our area. First, they showed us two

~~calfs~~ [calves] and three ~~sheeps~~ [sheep]. Then, they introduced us ~~too~~ [to] two ~~mans~~ [men] in costumes. The men

were making wooden ~~shelfs~~ [shelves] for the farmhouse and a rack ~~four~~ [for] the kitchen's ~~knifes~~ [knives]. We

also visited the cellar where ~~potatos~~ [potatoes], onions, and other vegetables were stored.

ERRORS: PLURALS: 13; HOMOPHONES: 6

94 Autumn Weekend at the Lake

To: anton@nomail.zap
From: brad@nomail.zap

Dear Anton,

Would you like ~~too~~ [to] come to the lake with us this weekend? Last time we went ~~their~~ [there], we

saw three ~~deers~~ [deer], two ~~oxes~~ [oxen], ~~fore~~ [four] mountain ~~sheeps~~ [sheep], and some wild ~~gooses~~ [geese]. Some ~~mans~~ [men]

said that they spotted a ~~pear~~ [pair] of ~~road fox~~ [red foxes] and a family of ~~wolfs~~ [wolves], but we did ~~knot~~ [not] see any.

This time of year is even better than summer. The leaves on the ~~tree~~ [trees] should be starting

to turn colors. We can take some beautiful ~~picture~~ [pictures]. Mom has planned a dinner with

salmon, baked ~~potatos~~ [potatoes], and a salad with ~~tomatos~~ [tomatoes]. Let me ~~no~~ [know] if you can come.

Your friend,
Brad

ERRORS: PLURALS: 11; HOMOPHONES: 7

Name: _____ Date: _____

Living History Farm 93 ✓

Today, hour class visited a living history farm. Many other class were there, sew the parking lot was full of school buses. First, we visited the pond. Some ducks and gooses waddled over to us on their flat, webbed foots. They wanted food, but we did not have any. Two womans met us at the museum building. They were wearing clothes from the pioneer period. They said that they were dressed as farm wifes. They explained that wee wood soon learn about the lifes of early farm family in our area. First, they showed us two calfs and three sheeps. Then, they introduced us too two mans in costumes. The men were making wooden shelfs for the farmhouse and a rack four the kitchen's knifes. We also visited the cellar where potatos, onions, and other vegetables were stored.

✓ MIXED REVIEW

Name: _____ Date: _____

Autumn Weekend at the Lake 94 ✓

To: anton@nomail.zap
From: brad@nomail.zap

Dear Anton,

Would you like too come to the lake with us this weekend? Last time we went their, we saw three deers, two oxes, fore mountain sheeps, and some wild gooses. Some mans said that they spotted a pear of read fox and a family of wolfs, but we did knot see any. This time of year is even better than summer. The leaves on the tree should be starting to turn colors. We can take some beautiful picture. Mom has planned a dinner with salmon, baked potatos, and a salad with tomatos. Let me no if you can come.

Your friend,
Brad

✓ MIXED REVIEW

95 **Running Track at the Park**

When James and Gavin arrived at the park, ~~he~~ [they] were out of breath. Since James was

competing in the first event, ~~she~~ [he] hurried to the track. Gavin found ~~their~~ [his] seat in the

stands. The runners took ~~his~~ [their] places at the starting line. Mr. Garrett, the referee, raised

~~their~~ [his] left arm, and then ~~she~~ [he] lowered it. ~~They~~ [He] said, "Go!" The boys sprang into action

and ran as fast as ~~he~~ [they] could. At first, James was behind, but ~~she~~ [he] quickly caught up.

~~They~~ [He] passed all of the other runners except Luis. Gavin stood up, and ~~they~~ [he] shouted,

"Run, James!" ~~They~~ [He] was excited when James edged past Luis. James took the lead,

and ~~she~~ [he] crossed the finish line first. Gavin rushed down to shake ~~their~~ [his] friend's hand

before taking ~~my~~ [his] own place on the track.

 ERRORS: PRONOUN/NOUN AGREEMENT: 15

---

96 **Harriet's Audition**

This afternoon, Felicia and I watched as ~~their~~ [our] friend Harriet climbed the steps to the

stage. ~~They~~ [We] both knew that Harriet's heart was pounding and ~~his~~ [her] knees were shaking.

It was ~~his~~ [her] turn to audition for the lead in the school play. All of the other girls had

already read ~~his~~ [their] parts. ~~She~~ [They] had done well. Harriet was nervous, but ~~he~~ [she] was ready.

We had helped her practice. When Harriet took ~~his~~ [her] place in front of the microphone,

Felicia and I cheered for her. Harriet's voice shook a little at first, but ~~he~~ [she] became more

confident as ~~they~~ [she] continued. ~~He~~ [She] really became the character. As soon as Harriet

finished, Felicia and I knew that ~~their~~ [our] friend would be chosen for the part. ~~He~~ [We] were

both very proud of her. ~~They~~ [We] took her to the ice cream shop to celebrate.

ERRORS: PRONOUN/NOUN AGREEMENT: 14

Name: _____ Date: _____

Running Track at the Park 95

When James and Gavin arrived at the park, he were out of breath. Since James was competing in the first event, she hurried to the track. Gavin found their seat in the stands. The runners took his places at the starting line. Mr. Garrett, the referee, raised their left arm, and then she lowered it. They said, "Go!" The boys sprang into action and ran as fast as he could. At first, James was behind, but she quickly caught up. They passed all of the other runners except Luis. Gavin stood up, and they shouted, "Run, James!" They was excited when James edged past Luis. James took the lead, and she crossed the finish line first. Gavin rushed down to shake their friend's hand before taking my own place on the track.

✔ LOOK FOR: PRONOUNS

Name: _____ Date: _____

Harriet's Audition 96

This afternoon, Felicia and I watched as their friend Harriet climbed the steps to the stage. They both knew that Harriet's heart was pounding and his knees were shaking. It was his turn to audition for the lead in the school play. All of the other girls had already read his parts. She had done well. Harriet was nervous, but he was ready. We had helped her practice. When Harriet took his place in front of the microphone, Felicia and I cheered for her. Harriet's voice shook a little at first, but he became more confident as they continued. He really became the character. As soon as Harriet finished, Felicia and I knew that their friend would be chosen for the part. He were both very proud of her. They took her to the ice cream shop to celebrate.

✔ LOOK FOR: PRONOUNS

97 · Shopping at the Mall

November 4, 2011

Dear Journal,

This morning, Jordana and ~~me~~ (I) went shopping. ~~She~~ (Her) mother picked me up in their family's van. Then, ~~her~~ (she) drove us to the mall. Jordana's little brother came too. ~~He~~ (His) name is Macon. ~~His~~ (He) will be five next month. First, ~~our~~ (we) went to Rose's Department Store, but ~~it~~ (its) doors were not open yet. Then, Jordana's mom and Macon wanted soft pretzels. ~~Their~~ (They) led the way to the shop. ~~Its~~ (It) was near the arcade. Jordana and ~~me~~ (I) played games while Macon and their mom ate. We had a good time. The next time ~~me~~ (my) mother goes to the mall, ~~me~~ (I) will invite Jordana. ~~We~~ (Our) car is not as big as a van, but ~~its~~ (it) has plenty of room.

✗ ERRORS: SUBJECT PRONOUNS: 9; POSSESSIVE PRONOUNS: 5

98 · Today at School

To: lonny@nomail.zap
From: erik@nomail.zap

Dear Lonny,

~~Our~~ (We) all missed you at school today. ~~My~~ (I) hope you will come tomorrow. Actually, ~~your~~ (you) were lucky to be home. Mr. Dorian was not happy with us. ~~His~~ (He) said that ~~our~~ (we) have not been turning in ~~we~~ (our) homework on time. Brittany raised ~~she~~ (her) hand. ~~Her~~ (She) said that she always did her work. Aaron rolled ~~he~~ (his) eyes. Most of us do ~~we~~ (our) work on time. Today, ~~my~~ (I) forgot ~~I~~ (my) backpack though. How embarrassing! I called Mom, and ~~her~~ (she) brought it. ~~My~~ (I) felt much better when ~~I~~ (my) homework was on Mr. Dorian's desk. Don't forget ~~you~~ (your) homework tomorrow!

Your friend,
Erik

✗ ERRORS: SUBJECT PRONOUNS: 9; POSSESSIVE PRONOUNS: 7

Name: _____ Date: _____

Shopping at the Mall (97)

November 4, 2011

Dear Journal,

This morning, Jordana and me went shopping. She mother picked me up in their family's van. Then, her drove us to the mall. Jordana's little brother came too. He name is Macon. His will be five next month. First, our went to Rose's Department Store, but it doors were not open yet. Then, Jordana's mom and Macon wanted soft pretzels. Their led the way to the shop. Its was near the arcade. Jordana and me played games while Macon and their mom ate. We had a good time. The next time me mother goes to the mall, me will invite Jordana. We car is not as big as a van, but its has plenty of room.

✔ LOOK FOR: SUBJECT PRONOUNS AND POSSESSIVE PRONOUNS

Name: _____ Date: _____

Today at School (98)

To: lonny@nomail.zap
From: erik@nomail.zap

Dear Lonny,

Our all missed you at school today. My hope you will come tomorrow. Actually, your were lucky to be home. Mr. Dorian was not happy with us. His said that our have not been turning in we homework on time. Brittany raised she hand. Her said that she always did her work. Aaron rolled he eyes. Most of us do we work on time. Today, my forgot I backpack though. How embarrassing! I called Mom, and her brought it. My felt much better when I homework was on Mr. Dorian's desk. Don't forget you homework tomorrow!

Your friend,
Erik

✔ LOOK FOR: SUBJECT PRONOUNS AND POSSESSIVE PRONOUNS

99 Craft Project

Danielle received some craft supplies for her birthday. She was working on a project

when Georgie, her little brother, came in. He pointed to a jar of paint.

"I like ~~those.~~ ^{that} Give ~~him~~ ^{it} to ~~I~~ ^{me}!" he demanded.

Danielle did not give it to ~~he.~~ ^{him} She pointed to the jar. "I'm sorry. ~~These~~ ^{This} is mine," she said.

Georgie pointed to some loose sheets of paper from her drawing pad on the other

side of the room. "Can I have some of ~~this~~ ^{that}?" he asked.

"Sure," Danielle said. She handed him three sheets of paper. "Now, ~~that~~ ^{these} sheets right

here are yours. You can draw on ~~they,~~ ^{them}" she said.

Georgie smiled. "Thank you," he said. Then, he took ~~they~~ ^{them} to his room.

Danielle smiled too. She picked up her project and started working on ~~us~~ ^{it} again.

ERRORS: OBJECT PRONOUNS: 6; DEMONSTRATIVE PRONOUNS: 4

100 Art Monitors

Katie and Eva are art monitors. Whenever Mrs. Kirk needs ~~him,~~ ^{them} Katie and Eva help ~~them.~~ ^{her}

Katie mixes the paint. Eva pours ~~them~~ ^{it} into containers. Katie collects the crayons. Eva

puts ~~they~~ ^{them} away. One day, Mrs. Kirk took some big sheets of paper out of the cabinet.

"~~This~~ ^{These} are for your winter paintings. Each student will need one," she said.

"I will pass ~~it~~ ^{them} out," Katie said.

She handed ~~they~~ ^{them} to Katie and walked to the front of the classroom. "Be careful with ~~those.~~ ^{those}

They're heavy," Mrs. Kirk warned as she walked out of the classroom.

Eva went to help Katie. "~~That~~ ^{Those} look hard to carry," she said. "Put ~~him~~ ^{them} down and let ~~I~~ ^{me} help you!"

Katie put down the papers. Each girl took some of ~~it.~~ ^{them} "~~These~~ ^{This} is an easy job for the two

of ~~we,~~ ^{us}" Eva said.

ERRORS: OBJECT PRONOUNS: 10; DEMONSTRATIVE PRONOUNS: 4

Name: _____ Date: _____

Craft Project (99)

Danielle received some craft supplies for her birthday. She was working on a project

when Georgie, her little brother, came in. He pointed to a jar of paint.

"I like those. Give him to I!" he demanded.

Danielle did not give it to he. She pointed to the jar. "I'm sorry. These is mine," she said.

Georgie pointed to some loose sheets of paper from her drawing pad on the other

side of the room. "Can I have some of this?" he asked.

"Sure," Danielle said. She handed him three sheets of paper. "Now, that sheets right

here are yours. You can draw on they," she said.

Georgie smiled. "Thank you," he said. Then, he took they to his room.

Danielle smiled too. She picked up her project and started working on us again.

✔ LOOK FOR: OBJECT PRONOUNS AND DEMONSTRATIVE PRONOUNS

Name: _____ Date: _____

Art Monitors (100)

Katie and Eva are art monitors. Whenever Mrs. Kirk needs him, Katie and Eva help them.

Katie mixes the paint. Eva pours them into containers. Katie collects the crayons. Eva

puts they away. One day, Mrs. Kirk took some big sheets of paper out of the cabinet.

"This are for your winter paintings. Each student will need one," she said.

"I will pass it out," Katie said.

She handed they to Katie and walked to the front of the classroom. "Be careful with these.

They're heavy," Mrs. Kirk warned as she walked out of the classroom.

Eva went to help Katie. "That look hard to carry," she said. "Put him down and let I help you!"

Katie put down the papers. Each girl took some of it. "These is an easy job for the two

of we," Eva said.

✔ LOOK FOR: OBJECT PRONOUNS AND DEMONSTRATIVE PRONOUNS

101 Planning a Party

September 21, 2010

Dear Journal,

I am worried. Is ~~anything~~ [anyone] coming to my party? Casey called to say that he will be

busy. Dante called too. He didn't want to be the only boy. I couldn't tell him which

boys were coming, so he said that he would stay home. The girls aren't any better.

~~Any~~ [Some] of them called yesterday. ~~Some~~ [All] of them said that they were busy. So far, ~~nothing~~ [no one]

is coming. ~~Somebody~~ [Everyone] has said no. I do not know what to do! I was looking for paper

cups for the party. There are ~~some~~ [none] left in the cupboard—not even one! I was planning

to buy ~~any~~ [some] before Saturday, but now I am not sure if I will need ~~some~~ [any].

ERRORS: INDEFINITE PRONOUNS: 8

102 Art in Our Class

All of the students in our class like art. There is no one in our room ~~whom~~ [who] does not like

it. There are many types of art projects; it is hard to say ~~who~~ [which] is the most popular. Some

people like painting the best. Others like clay, ~~that~~ [which] is very flexible. Almost all of the

students like crafts. A few people are good at drawing; we all know ~~whom~~ [who] they are.

~~Whomever~~ [Whoever] does the best job is famous for the afternoon. At the end of the lesson,

the students walk around to see all of the pictures ~~when~~ [that] have been created that day.

Some are better than others, but all of them are creative. The important thing is ~~which~~ [that]

everyone has fun!

ERRORS: RELATIVE PRONOUNS: 7

Name: _____ Date: _____

Planning a Party (101)

September 21, 2010

Dear Journal,

I am worried. Is anything coming to my party? Casey called to say that he will be busy. Dante called too. He didn't want to be the only boy. I couldn't tell him which boys were coming, so he said that he would stay home. The girls aren't any better. Any of them called yesterday. Some of them said that they were busy. So far, nothing is coming. Somebody has said no. I do not know what to do! I was looking for paper cups for the party. There are some left in the cupboard—not even one! I was planning to buy any before Saturday, but now I am not sure if I will need some.

✔ LOOK FOR: INDEFINITE PRONOUNS

Name: _____ Date: _____

Art in Our Class (102)

All of the students in our class like art. There is no one in our room whom does not like it. There are many types of art projects; it is hard to say who is the most popular. Some people like painting the best. Others like clay, that is very flexible. Almost all of the students like crafts. A few people are good at drawing; we all know whom they are. Whomever does the best job is famous for the afternoon. At the end of the lesson, the students walk around to see all of the pictures when have been created that day. Some are better than others, but all of them are creative. The important thing is which everyone has fun!

✔ LOOK FOR: RELATIVE PRONOUNS

103   Art Club Memo

Dear Craft Club Members,

Whoever
~~Whomever~~ forgot to return the scissors should bring ~~it~~ *them* back to the art room. A few pairs

were missing from the set after our meeting. The second graders will need ~~they~~ *them* tomorrow.

no one
In the future, ~~someone~~ will be allowed to remove supplies from the room. The school

us   *we*   *we*   *it*   *I*
trusts ~~we~~, and ~~us~~ have a responsibility to leave the workspace as ~~our~~ found ~~them~~. ~~Me~~ am

this
sure that ~~these~~ was a mistake. The culprits probably do not even know ~~whom~~ *who* they are.

his   *her*
That is why I am asking each member to check ~~he~~ or ~~she~~ backpack. The scissors are easy

they   *them*   *your*
to see; ~~them~~ have yellow handles. Call me if you find ~~they~~. Thank you for ~~you~~ help!

Your president,
Liz

> ✖ ERRORS: SUBECT PRONOUNS: 4; POSSESSIVE PRONOUNS: 3; OBJECT PRONOUNS: 5;
> DEMONSTRATIVE PRONOUNS: 1; INDEFINITE PRONOUNS: 1; RELATIVE PRONOUNS: 2

104   Family Reunion

To: jack@nomail.zap
From: jerry@nomail.zap

Dear Jack,

our   *my*   *who*
We went to ~~us~~ family reunion yesterday. I finally met ~~I~~ cousin, ~~whom~~ lives in Ontario.

Her   *she*   *I*   *her*
~~She~~ name is Julie, and ~~her~~ is almost a year younger than ~~me~~ am. I liked ~~she~~ very

which
much. The reunion was held in a big park. There was a large lake, ~~who~~ was filled with

I   *them*
friendly ducks and geese. Julie and ~~me~~ bought some corn and fed it to ~~they~~. We are

My
planning to write to each other from now on. ~~Me~~ family might even go to Ontario next

she   *I*   *her*
summer. Maybe ~~her~~ will visit our house too. ~~Me~~ would like for you to meet ~~she~~.

Your
~~You~~ friend,
Jerry

> ✖ ERRORS: PRONOUN/NOUN AGREEMENT: 1; SUBECT PRONOUNS: 4;
> POSSESSIVE PRONOUNS: 5; OBJECT PRONOUNS: 3; RELATIVE PRONOUNS: 2

Name: _____ Date: _____

Art Club Memo 103

Dear Craft Club Members,

Whomever forgot to return the scissors should bring it back to the art room. A few pairs

were missing from the set after our meeting. The second graders will need they tomorrow.

In the future, someone will be allowed to remove supplies from the room. The school

trusts we, and us have a responsibility to leave the workspace as our found them. Me am

sure that these was a mistake. The culprits probably do not even know whom they are.

That is why I am asking each member to check he or she backpack. The scissors are easy

to see; them have yellow handles. Call me if you find they. Thank you for you help!

Your president,
Liz

✓ MIXED REVIEW

Name: _____ Date: _____

Family Reunion 104

To: jack@nomail.zap
From: jerry@nomail.zap

Dear Jack,

We went to us family reunion yesterday. I finally met I cousin, whom lives in Ontario.

She name is Julie, and her is almost a year younger than me am. I liked she very

much. The reunion was held in a big park. There was a large lake, who was filled with

friendly ducks and geese. Julie and me bought some corn and fed it to they. We are

planning to write to each other from now on. Me family might even go to Ontario next

summer. Maybe her will visit our house too. Me would like for you to meet she.

You friend,
Jerry

✓ MIXED REVIEW

105 Valerie's Afternoon

After school, Valerie ~~lay~~ [laid] her backpack on a chair by her desk and ~~laid~~ [lay] down on the bed. It felt good just to ~~lay~~ [lie] there. Her eyes were tired, so she closed them and listened to the noises of the afternoon. Outside of her window ~~laid~~ [lay] the busy city, but the sounds of traffic did not bother her. In the nearby hallway, her neighbor Marilyn was ~~sitting~~ [setting] an advertising flyer in front of each apartment's door. Valerie heard her as she walked, humming, toward the elevator. Once, Valerie had walked beside her, and Marilyn told her about a film role she wanted. Replaying that day in her mind, Valerie fell asleep and dreamed about being a movie star. She had ~~laid~~ [lain] there for about two hours when her mom called her for dinner. She ~~raised~~ [rose] quickly, wondering what had happened to the afternoon.

ERRORS: TRANSITIVE/INTRANSITIVE VERBS: 7

106 Exercise Class

Today, Tia started an exercise class. Ruby and I were her first students. First, we ~~sat~~ [set] our bags near the wall and ~~lay~~ [laid] our mats on the floor. When she saw that we were ready, Tia told us to ~~rise~~ [raise] our hands high over our heads and stretch. Next, we ~~laid~~ [lay] down on the mats and ~~rised~~ [raised] our legs one at a time. After that, we ~~raised~~ [rose] up slowly to a sitting position. We ~~set~~ [sat] there and rested until Tia told us to ~~lay~~ [lie] down again. This time, we ~~rose~~ [raised] our arms above our heads and rolled forward. By the time we ~~raised~~ [rose] all of the way up, I was worn-out. Next, Tia ~~sat~~ [set] a huge plastic ball in front of each of us. I just ~~set~~ [sat] down and stared at it. I was exhausted.

ERRORS: TRANSITIVE/INTRANSITIVE VERBS: 12

Name: _____ Date: _____

Valerie's Afternoon 105

After school, Valerie lay her backpack on a chair by her desk and laid down on the bed. It felt good just to lay there. Her eyes were tired, so she closed them and listened to the noises of the afternoon. Outside of her window laid the busy city, but the sounds of traffic did not bother her. In the nearby hallway, her neighbor Marilyn was sitting an advertising flyer in front of each apartment's door. Valerie heard her as she walked, humming, toward the elevator. Once, Valerie had walked beside her, and Marilyn told her about a film role she wanted. Replaying that day in her mind, Valerie fell asleep and dreamed about being a movie star. She had laid there for about two hours when her mom called her for dinner. She raised quickly, wondering what had happened to the afternoon.

✔ LOOK FOR: TRANSITIVE AND INTRANSITIVE VERBS

Name: _____ Date: _____

Exercise Class 106

Today, Tia started an exercise class. Ruby and I were her first students. First, we sat our bags near the wall and lay our mats on the floor. When she saw that we were ready, Tia told us to rise our hands high over our heads and stretch. Next, we laid down on the mats and rised our legs one at a time. After that, we raised up slowly to a sitting position. We set there and rested until Tia told us to lay down again. This time, we rose our arms above our heads and rolled forward. By the time we raised all of the way up, I was worn-out. Next, Tia sat a huge plastic ball in front of each of us. I just set down and stared at it. I was exhausted.

✔ LOOK FOR: TRANSITIVE AND INTRANSITIVE VERBS

107 Science Project Cooperation

Abel and I ~~has work~~ *have worked* on our science project for a week. By the time we finish, we will ~~has~~ *have* read at least five books. I ~~has be~~ *have been* lucky to have such a good partner. Before we began, Abel already ~~have check~~ *had checked* some Web sites. Also, he ~~have write~~ *had written* some questions for us to answer in our report. Those questions ~~has be~~ *have been* very helpful. He and I ~~has look~~ *have looked* for books in the library together. I ~~has learn~~ *have learned* a lot about research from him. By the time we turn in our report, he will ~~has learn~~ *have learned* a lot about drawing from me. I ~~has draw~~ *have drawn* most of the pictures, but Abel ~~have make~~ *has made* the charts. He ~~have do~~ *has done* some good drawings too.

✗ ERRORS: PERFECT TENSE VERBS: PAST: 2; PRESENT: 8; FUTURE: 2

108 Checkers for Charity

Before today, Ellen ~~have~~ *had* never ~~play~~ *played* checkers in her life. By 5:00 P.M. on Sunday, two days from now, she and her friend Carrie will ~~has play~~ *have played* more than 50 games. Twenty other members of the Springville Service Club will also ~~has spend~~ *have spent* the weekend facing checkerboards. The annual Checkers Marathon ~~have raise~~ *has raised* money for the local homeless center for many years. It ~~have became~~ *has become* a local tradition. Each team ~~have find~~ *has found* at least one sponsor. The sponsors ~~has promise~~ *have promised* to make a donation for each game completed. By the end of the event, the service club will ~~has raise~~ *have raised* enough money to buy several new beds for the shelter.

✗ ERRORS: PERFECT TENSE VERBS: PAST: 1; PRESENT: 4; FUTURE: 3

Name: _____ Date: _____

Science Project Cooperation (107)

Abel and I has work on our science project for a week. By the time we finish, we will has read at least five books. I has be lucky to have such a good partner. Before we began, Abel already have check some Web sites. Also, he have write some questions for us to answer in our report. Those questions has be very helpful. He and I has look for books in the library together. I has learn a lot about research from him. By the time we turn in our report, he will has learn a lot about drawing from me. I has draw most of the pictures, but Abel have make the charts. He have do some good drawings too.

LOOK FOR: PERFECT TENSE VERBS

Name: _____ Date: _____

Checkers for Charity (108)

Before today, Ellen have never play checkers in her life. By 5:00 P.M. on Sunday, two days from now, she and her friend Carrie will has play more than 50 games. Twenty other members of the Springville Service Club will also has spend the weekend facing checkerboards. The annual Checkers Marathon have raise money for the local homeless center for many years. It have became a local tradition. Each team have find at least one sponsor. The sponsors has promise to make a donation for each game completed. By the end of the event, the service club will has raise enough money to buy several new beds for the shelter.

LOOK FOR: PERFECT TENSE VERBS

109 · A Close Call

The wind ~~blowed~~ (blew) all night long. The whole house ~~shaked~~ (shook). When the sun ~~rised~~ (rose), Mom,

Dad, and I ~~goed~~ (went) into the yard to look around. We ~~knowed~~ (knew) that it was going to be

a mess, but we were not ready for what we ~~seed~~ (saw). One of the big oak tree's boughs

had broken and fallen down. A heavy limb ~~catched~~ (caught) on the roof of the garage and

pulled half of it down. What a mess! Dad ~~cutted~~ (cut) up part of the fallen tree. Mom and

I dragged the pieces out of the driveway. Then, Dad carefully ~~drived~~ (drove) the car out of

the garage. We ~~quitted~~ (quit) working at about 10:00 A.M. and ~~eated~~ (ate) breakfast on the patio.

Next week, a tree service will come to haul the rest of the branches away. Thank

goodness our house was ~~builded~~ (built) far enough away from that tree. We ~~losed~~ (lost) a few

shingles from the roof, but everything else seemed fine.

ERRORS: IRREGULAR PAST TENSE VERBS: 13

110 · Bird-Watching

Hugo and I ~~builded~~ (built) a birdhouse last weekend. We ~~putted~~ (put) it on the back fence. We

also ~~hanged~~ (hung) a hummingbird feeder. Then, we ~~eated~~ (ate) our lunch in the yard so that

we could watch our guests arrive. Three sparrows ~~comed~~ (came) to look at the birdhouse.

Two of them ~~sitted~~ (sat) on the roof and ~~singed~~ (sang) for a while, but none of them stayed. The

hummingbirds liked the feeder. They ~~drinked~~ (drank) a lot of the sweet, red nectar. Most of them

~~fighted~~ (fought) with each other. One mean bird ~~thinked~~ (thought) the feeder belonged to him, and he

~~drived~~ (drove) away all of the others. When he buzzed by, the feeder ~~shaked~~ (shook) and nectar dripped

on the ground. While the king of the feeder was busy chasing competitors away, a smart

little hummingbird ~~hided~~ (hid) on the other side of the bottle and ~~stealed~~ (stole) some forbidden

juice. Then, he ~~flied~~ (flew) away. The mean bird never ~~catched~~ (caught) him. Hugo and I cheered.

ERRORS: IRREGULAR PAST TENSE VERBS: 16

Name: _____ Date: _____

A Close Call 109

The wind blowed all night long. The whole house shaked. When the sun rised, Mom,
Dad, and I goed into the yard to look around. We knowed that it was going to be
a mess, but we were not ready for what we seed. One of the big oak tree's boughs
had broken and fallen down. A heavy limb catched on the roof of the garage and
pulled half of it down. What a mess! Dad cutted up part of the fallen tree. Mom and
I dragged the pieces out of the driveway. Then, Dad carefully drived the car out of
the garage. We quitted working at about 10:00 A.M. and eated breakfast on the patio.
Next week, a tree service will come to haul the rest of the branches away. Thank
goodness our house was builded far enough away from that tree. We losed a few
shingles from the roof, but everything else seemed fine.

✔ LOOK FOR: IRREGULAR PAST TENSE VERBS

Name: _____ Date: _____

Bird-Watching 110

Hugo and I builded a birdhouse last weekend. We putted it on the back fence. We
also hanged a hummingbird feeder. Then, we eated our lunch in the yard so that
we could watch our guests arrive. Three sparrows comed to look at the birdhouse.
Two of them sitted on the roof and singed for a while, but none of them stayed. The
hummingbirds liked the feeder. They drinked a lot of the sweet, red nectar. Most of them
fighted with each other. One mean bird thinked the feeder belonged to him, and he
drived away all of the others. When he buzzed by, the feeder shaked and nectar dripped
on the ground. While the king of the feeder was busy chasing competitors away, a smart
little hummingbird hided on the other side of the bottle and stealed some forbidden
juice. Then, he flied away. The mean bird never catched him. Hugo and I cheered.

✔ LOOK FOR: IRREGULAR PAST TENSE VERBS

111 Mr. Christopher's Class

My name ~~was~~ [is] Carl. My friend Darrell and I ~~be~~ [are] in the fifth grade. Finally, we ~~be~~ [are]

in the same class. We ~~are~~ [were] both excited when we found out. Darrell and I have ~~be~~ [been] in

different classes since second grade. I ~~was~~ [am] glad we ~~be~~ [are] together now. Our teacher ~~was~~ [is]

Mr. Christopher. I ~~been~~ [am] sure we ~~were~~ [are] the luckiest students in the school. Mr. Christopher

~~is~~ [was] my brother's teacher two years ago. My brother thought he ~~is~~ [was] great, and I can see

why. Every day, Mr. Christopher always ~~seemed~~ [seems] so happy. It ~~was~~ [is] easy to see that he

loves his job. So far, this has ~~be~~ [been] my best year ever!

ERRORS: IRREGULAR LINKING VERBS: 15

112 Class President

This morning, Alfonso ~~becomed~~ [became] our new class president. In our classroom, there

~~be~~ [are] many jobs. There ~~were~~ [is] a job for every student. Best of all, everybody gets to be

president for a week. Everyone usually ~~seemed~~ [seems] happy about that. Ebony ~~is~~ [was] president

last week. Next week, Byron will ~~been~~ [be] president. Each day, the president ~~was~~ [is] the

one who dismisses the class for recess and lunch. The president ~~be~~ [is] also the office

monitor. I have ~~be~~ [been] a team captain, an art monitor, and a book monitor. Soon, I will

~~been~~ [be] the president. It will ~~felt~~ [feel] good to be a leader. Maybe I will ~~been~~ [be] a mayor or a

governor someday.

ERRORS: IRREGULAR LINKING VERBS: 12

Name: _____ Date: _____

Mr. Christopher's Class 111

My name was Carl. My friend Darrell and I be in the fifth grade. Finally, we be

in the same class. We are both excited when we found out. Darrell and I have be in

different classes since second grade. I was glad we be together now. Our teacher was

Mr. Christopher. I been sure we were the luckiest students in the school. Mr. Christopher

is my brother's teacher two years ago. My brother thought he is great, and I can see

why. Every day, Mr. Christopher always seemed so happy. It was easy to see that he

loves his job. So far, this has be my best year ever!

✔ LOOK FOR: IRREGULAR LINKING VERBS

Name: _____ Date: _____

Class President 112

This morning, Alfonso becomed our new class president. In our classroom, there

be many jobs. There were a job for every student. Best of all, everybody gets to be

president for a week. Everyone usually seemed happy about that. Ebony is president

last week. Next week, Byron will been president. Each day, the president was the

one who dismisses the class for recess and lunch. The president be also the office

monitor. I have be a team captain, an art monitor, and a book monitor. Soon, I will

been the president. It will felt good to be a leader. Maybe I will been a mayor or a

governor someday.

✔ LOOK FOR: IRREGULAR LINKING VERBS

113 Monday Math Challenge

Every Monday, students in Mrs. Verdan's class ~~works~~ *work* with partners to complete math

challenges. Each pair ~~select~~ *selects* its own working space. Jeremy and Melvin ~~goes~~ *go* to

the math center. Gregory and Leo ~~likes~~ *like* the sunny table by the window. Henry and

Jeff ~~chooses~~ *choose* chairs near the whiteboard. Lily and Masandra ~~takes~~ *take* the round table

near the door. Mandy and Zoe ~~grabs~~ *grab* the soft seats in the library corner. Macon and

Travis ~~sits~~ *sit* near the science center. All of the pairs ~~has~~ *have* forty-five minutes to solve the

day's puzzle. Most of them ~~finishes~~ *finish* on time. They ~~shares~~ *share* their solutions with the whole

group. A few ~~meets~~ *meet* with Mrs. Verdan after school. She ~~explain~~ *explains* the solution and ~~answer~~ *answers*

questions. Mrs. Verdan's students always ~~enjoys~~ *enjoy* the weekly math challenges.

ERRORS: SUBJECT/VERB AGREEMENT: 15

114 Game Day

Once a month, our school ~~hold~~ *holds* a game day on the playground. We ~~participates~~ *participate* in

races and other games. Our teachers ~~gives~~ *give* the winners blue ribbons. Fernando and

Melvin always ~~races~~ *race* on the same team. Sometimes they win, and other times they ~~loses~~ *lose*,

but they always ~~enjoys~~ *enjoy* running. Target toss ~~are~~ *is* a favorite event. Each player ~~toss~~ *tosses* the ball

at a target painted on the wall. Laura and Jordana usually ~~wins~~ *win* because they ~~practices~~ *practice*

after school. Jose and Luke ~~likes~~ *like* basketball. Kyle and Spencer usually ~~scores~~ *score* more points,

but Jose and Luke ~~is~~ *are* improving all of the time. Sometimes, they ~~takes~~ *take* home the prize.

At the end of the day, teams from two classes ~~plays~~ *play* a game of volleyball. Everybody

~~watch~~ *watches* and ~~cheer~~ *cheers* for his side. The winning team ~~coach~~ *coaches* the fourth graders for a week.

ERRORS: SUBJECT/VERB AGREEMENT: 18

Name: _____   Date: _____

Monday Math Challenge (113)

Every Monday, students in Mrs. Verdan's class works with partners to complete math challenges. Each pair select its own working space. Jeremy and Melvin goes to the math center. Gregory and Leo likes the sunny table by the window. Henry and Jeff chooses chairs near the whiteboard. Lily and Masandra takes the round table near the door. Mandy and Zoe grabs the soft seats in the library corner. Macon and Travis sits near the science center. All of the pairs has forty-five minutes to solve the day's puzzle. Most of them finishes on time. They shares their solutions with the whole group. A few meets with Mrs. Verdan after school. She explain the solution and answer questions. Mrs. Verdan's students always enjoys the weekly math challenges.

✔ LOOK FOR: VERBS

Name: _____   Date: _____

Game Day (114)

Once a month, our school hold a game day on the playground. We participates in races and other games. Our teachers gives the winners blue ribbons. Fernando and Melvin always races on the same team. Sometimes they win, and other times they loses, but they always enjoys running. Target toss are a favorite event. Each player toss the ball at a target painted on the wall. Laura and Jordana usually wins because they practices after school. Jose and Luke likes basketball. Kyle and Spencer usually scores more points, but Jose and Luke is improving all of the time. Sometimes, they takes home the prize. At the end of the day, teams from two classes plays a game of volleyball. Everybody watch and cheer for his side. The winning team coach the fourth graders for a week.

✔ LOOK FOR: VERBS

115   Walking to School

                   are   have walked

Davetta and Natalie ~~is~~ best friends. They ~~has walk~~ to school together since

                              knocks

kindergarten. Every day, Davetta ~~knock~~ on Natalie's door at exactly 7:30 A.M. Usually,

      has been   has been

Natalie ~~have be~~ right there waiting to greet her friend, but a few times she ~~have be~~

           had watched   was

late. Once, she ~~has watch~~ a movie until 11:00 P.M. the night before, so she ~~is~~ still

                                         rose

sleeping peacefully when her confused friend called. Natalie ~~raised~~ from her bed

                              laid   sat

and dressed as fast as she could. Davetta just ~~lay~~ down her backpack and ~~set~~ on the

porch steps to wait. She and Natalie laughed about it all of the way to school. The girls

                           leave   have walked

figured out that by the time they ~~leaves~~ Forest Elementary, they will ~~had walk~~ to school

together more than 1,000 times!

> **ERRORS: TRANSITIVE/INTRANSITIVE VERBS: 3; PERFECT TENSE VERBS: 5; IRREGULAR LINKING VERBS: 1; SUBJECT/VERB AGREEMENT: 3**

116   Boys and Bikes

                    live   have owned

Neil and Gerardo ~~lives~~ in the country. Their families ~~has own~~ and operated neighboring

                                                were

ranches for generations. Their fathers have been friends since they ~~was~~ boys, and their

          knew   were   have gone

mothers ~~knowed~~ each other long before they ~~was~~ married. Neil and Gerardo ~~has go~~ to

                                                bought

school together for as long as they can remember. Last year, their parents ~~buyed~~ them

                                         spent

matching mountain bikes. Since then, they have ~~spended~~ every sunny weekend in the

             have challenged   are

hills. Neil and Gerardo ~~has challenge~~ each other to improve, and now they ~~be~~ the best

riders in the region. They plan to compete in the state championships next summer.

          is

Everybody ~~be~~ hoping that they will come home with first place trophies.

> **ERRORS: PERFECT TENSE VERBS: 3; IRREGULAR PAST TENSE VERBS: 3; IRREGULAR LINKING VERBS: 2; SUBJECT/VERB AGREEMENT: 3**

Name: _____ Date: _____

Walking to School (115)

Davetta and Natalie is best friends. They has walk to school together since

kindergarten. Every day, Davetta knock on Natalie's door at exactly 7:30 A.M. Usually,

Natalie have be right there waiting to greet her friend, but a few times she have be

late. Once, she has watch a movie until 11:00 P.M. the night before, so she is still

sleeping peacefully when her confused friend called. Natalie raised from her bed

and dressed as fast as she could. Davetta just lay down her backpack and set on the

porch steps to wait. She and Natalie laughed about it all of the way to school. The girls

figured out that by the time they leaves Forest Elementary, they will had walk to school

together more than 1,000 times!

✔ MIXED REVIEW

Name: _____ Date: _____

Boys and Bikes (116)

Neil and Gerardo lives in the country. Their families has own and operated neighboring

ranches for generations. Their fathers have been friends since they was boys, and their

mothers knowed each other long before they was married. Neil and Gerardo has go to

school together for as long as they can remember. Last year, their parents buyed them

matching mountain bikes. Since then, they have spended every sunny weekend in the

hills. Neil and Gerardo has challenge each other to improve, and now they be the best

riders in the region. They plan to compete in the state championships next summer.

Everybody be hoping that they will come home with first place trophies.

✔ MIXED REVIEW

117 — Mosaics

A mosaic is a special kind ~~to~~ *of* picture or design. A mosaic can hang ~~off~~ *on* a wall, or it can be part ~~above~~ *of* a floor. The artist uses pieces of stone, tile, paper, or colorful glass instead of paint. First, the artist plans her picture ~~under~~ *on* a sheet of paper, and she fixes all of the mistakes. Then, she draws her plan again ~~under~~ *on* top of a piece of wood or another strong backing. She glues colorful pieces ~~off~~ *onto* the correct areas ~~to~~ *of* the picture. For example, she might glue blue stones or tiles ~~during~~ *onto* the picture of the sky, or she might glue pink tile ~~against~~ *onto* a picture of a flower. When she finishes, the artist puts special plaster, called *grout*, ~~near~~ *between* the pieces. There are many famous mosaics ~~toward~~ *in* museums around the world.

ERRORS: PREPOSITIONS: 11

118 — Mirrors

You look in a mirror, ~~but~~ *and* you see yourself. It happens every day, ~~and~~ *but* what is really happening? Light rays go into the silvery mirror, ~~yet~~ *and* then they bounce straight back to your eyes. That kind of mirror is flat, ~~yet~~ *and* it is called a *plane mirror*. There are two other kinds of mirrors: *convex* ~~but~~ *and* *concave*. It is easy to see how they work. Find a shiny silver (or stainless steel) spoon, ~~but~~ *and* look at yourself in the curved back. It is a convex surface. Your eyes look smaller, ~~so~~ *but* your nose looks bigger. A convex mirror curves outward. The light rays bounce off of it at an angle ~~or~~ *and* do not come straight back to your eye. Now, look at the bowl of the spoon. It is a concave surface. A concave mirror turns your face upside down. Why do you think this happens?

ERRORS: CONJUNCTIONS: 8

Name: _____ Date: _____

Mosaics 117

A mosaic is a special kind to picture or design. A mosaic can hang off a wall, or it can be part above a floor. The artist uses pieces of stone, tile, paper, or colorful glass instead of paint. First, the artist plans her picture under a sheet of paper, and she fixes all of the mistakes. Then, she draws her plan again under top of a piece of wood or another strong backing. She glues colorful pieces off the correct areas to the picture. For example, she might glue blue stones or tiles during the picture of the sky, or she might glue pink tile against a picture of a flower. When she finishes, the artist puts special plaster, called *grout*, near the pieces. There are many famous mosaics toward museums around the world.

✔ LOOK FOR: PREPOSITIONS

Name: _____ Date: _____

Mirrors 118

You look in a mirror, but you see yourself. It happens every day, and what is really happening? Light rays go into the silvery mirror, yet then they bounce straight back to your eyes. That kind of mirror is flat, yet it is called a *plane mirror*. There are two other kinds of mirrors: *convex* but *concave*. It is easy to see how they work. Find a shiny silver (or stainless steel) spoon, but look at yourself in the curved back. It is a convex surface. Your eyes look smaller, so your nose looks bigger. A convex mirror curves outward. The light rays bounce off of it at an angle or do not come straight back to your eye. Now, look at the bowl of the spoon. It is a concave surface. A concave mirror turns your face upside down. Why do you think this happens?

✔ LOOK FOR: CONJUNCTIONS

119 Camping by the Lake

This is the ~~prettier~~ [prettiest] campground I have ever seen. The trees are ~~tallest~~ [taller] and ~~oldest~~ [older] than

the ones in the valley. The campground is ~~farthest~~ [farther] away from the highway than the

one we stayed at last year, so it is much ~~quietest~~ [quieter]. It is a little ~~smallest~~ [smaller] than that one

too, so there are ~~fewest~~ [fewer] people. Our campsite is ~~closest~~ [closer] to the lake than to the woods.

Dad says that at night, the moon will be ~~brightest~~ [brighter] and the stars will be ~~easiest~~ [easier] to see

than they would be under the trees. This afternoon, we hiked on a path beside the

lake because it was ~~straightest~~ [straighter] and ~~flat~~ [flatter] than the trail to Evans Peak. My brother was

~~bravest~~ [braver] than I was. He took a much ~~hardest~~ [harder] route than I did. I was ~~smartest~~ [smarter] than he

was though. I returned to camp a half hour ~~soon~~ [sooner] than he did. Because his route was

~~difficulter~~ [more difficult], he went much ~~slowest~~ [slower] than I did on the regular trail.

✗ ERRORS: COMPARATIVE/SUPERLATIVE ADJECTIVES: 18

120 Springtime

Spring is drawing ~~closest~~ [closer] every day. I think it is the ~~lovlier~~ [lovliest] season of the year. It is

~~warmest~~ [warmer] every day, and the sky gets ~~brightest~~ [brighter] ~~earliest~~ [earlier] every morning. The sun rises

~~soonest~~ [sooner], and it sets ~~latest~~ [later] every afternoon. There is much ~~most~~ [more] time to ride my bicycle

with my friends after school. Spring is the year's ~~busier~~ [busiest] season at our house; we clean

every room and plant the garden. I love to watch the neighborhood turn green a little

at a time. The birds seem ~~cheerfuller~~ [more cheerful] too. Their songs are ~~loudest~~ [louder] and ~~sweet~~ [sweeter] than they

are at any other time of the year. In fact, two little birds are building a nest in the tree

in front of our house. They are even ~~busy~~ [busier] than we are!

✗ ERRORS: COMPARATIVE/SUPERLATIVE ADJECTIVES: 13

Name: _____ Date: _____

Camping by the Lake (119)

This is the prettier campground I have ever seen. The trees are tallest and oldest than the ones in the valley. The campground is farthest away from the highway than the one we stayed at last year, so it is much quietest. It is a little smallest than that one too, so there are fewest people. Our campsite is closest to the lake than to the woods. Dad says that at night, the moon will be brightest and the stars will be easiest to see than they would be under the trees. This afternoon, we hiked on a path beside the lake because it was straightest and flat than the trail to Evans Peak. My brother was bravest than I was. He took a much hardest route than I did. I was smartest than he was though. I returned to camp a half hour soon than he did. Because his route was difficulter, he went much slowest than I did on the regular trail.

✔ LOOK FOR: COMPARING ADJECTIVES

....

Name: _____ Date: _____

Springtime (120)

Spring is drawing closest every day. I think it is the lovlier season of the year. It is warmest every day, and the sky gets brightest earliest every morning. The sun rises soonest, and it sets latest every afternoon. There is much most time to ride my bicycle with my friends after school. Spring is the year's busier season at our house; we clean every room and plant the garden. I love to watch the neighborhood turn green a little at a time. The birds seem cheerfuller too. Their songs are loudest and sweet than they are at any other time of the year. In fact, two little birds are building a nest in the tree in front of our house. They are even busy than we are!

✔ LOOK FOR: COMPARING ADJECTIVES

121 · The Performance

Michael walked ~~brisk~~ (briskly) down the hall. His heart pounded ~~loud~~ (loudly) in his ears. He stood in front of the door for ~~exact~~ (exactly) one minute. Then, he ~~brave~~ (bravely) turned the knob and ~~slow~~ (slowly) pushed the door open. He slipped ~~quiet~~ (quietly) into the auditorium. Kenneth, Marty, and Zack were already sitting on the stage. They were looking around ~~anxious~~ (anxiously). When they spotted him, they waved ~~enthusiastic~~ (enthusiastically). ~~Quick~~ (Quickly), he made his way down the aisle, ~~successful~~ (successfully) ignoring the audience. Kenneth handed him his case. Michael released the catches and lifted out his trumpet. He nodded to Mrs. Nichols ~~confident~~ (confidently), and she introduced them. He ~~easy~~ (easily) lifted the horn to his lips and began to play. ~~Amazing~~ (Amazingly), once he started, all of his fears disappeared. Later, everyone told him how ~~good~~ (well) he played, and he ~~absolute~~ (absolutely) enjoyed the compliments. But, something else was more important to him; he had ~~temporary~~ (temporarily) conquered his stage fright.

✗ ERRORS: ADVERBS: 16

---

122 · Motion on the Moon

On August 2, 1971, Commander David R. Scott stood ~~proud~~ (proudly) on the surface of the moon. As the camera rolled ~~steady~~ (steadily), the astronaut ~~dramatic~~ (dramatically) dropped two ~~complete~~ (completely) ordinary things. One of them was a falcon feather, and the other was a hammer. In most places on Earth, the hammer would fall much ~~fast~~ (faster). ~~Amazing~~ (Amazingly), the two objects landed ~~gentle~~ (gently) on the moon's surface at ~~near~~ (nearly) the same time. ~~Unbelievable~~ (Unbelievably), Galileo Galilei had ~~accurate~~ (accurately) predicted the results of this experiment ~~near~~ (nearly) 400 years earlier. Galileo ~~scientific~~ (scientifically) designed experiments to develop his ideas about motion. A legend claims that the famous astronomer ~~bold~~ (boldly) dropped a cannonball and a musket ball from the Leaning Tower of Pisa to test his theory. Few modern historians ~~actual~~ (actually) believe the tale, but none question the fact that Galileo experimented with falling objects.

✗ ERRORS: ADVERBS: 14

Name: _____ Date: _____

The Performance 121

Michael walked brisk down the hall. His heart pounded loud in his ears. He stood in front of the door for exact one minute. Then, he brave turned the knob and slow pushed the door open. He slipped quiet into the auditorium. Kenneth, Marty, and Zack were already sitting on the stage. They were looking around anxious. When they spotted him, they waved enthusiastic. Quick, he made his way down the aisle, successful ignoring the audience. Kenneth handed him his case. Michael released the catches and lifted out his trumpet. He nodded to Mrs. Nichols confident, and she introduced them. He easy lifted the horn to his lips and began to play. Amazing, once he started, all of his fears disappeared. Later, everyone told him how good he played, and he absolute enjoyed the compliments. But, something else was more important to him; he had temporary conquered his stage fright.

✔ LOOK FOR: ADVERBS

Name: _____ Date: _____

Motion on the Moon 122

On August 2, 1971, Commander David R. Scott stood proud on the surface of the moon. As the camera rolled steady, the astronaut dramatic dropped two complete ordinary things. One of them was a falcon feather, and the other was a hammer. In most places on Earth, the hammer would fall much fast. Amazing, the two objects landed gentle on the moon's surface at near the same time. Unbelievable, Galileo Galilei had accurate predicted the results of this experiment near 400 years earlier. Galileo scientific designed experiments to develop his ideas about motion. A legend claims that the famous astronomer bold dropped a cannonball and a musket ball from the Leaning Tower of Pisa to test his theory. Few modern historians actual believe the tale, but none question the fact that Galileo experimented with falling objects.

✔ LOOK FOR: ADVERBS

123 My Cousin Jeff

My cousin Jeff is ~~oldest~~ [older] than I am, ~~but~~ [and] he is taller too. He shoots baskets ~~amazing good~~ [amazingly well], but I still win many ~~to~~ [of] our games. Jeff does not shoot as ~~accurate~~ [accurately] as I do. He tosses the ball too ~~quick~~ [quickly]. It hits the rim, ~~but~~ [and] it does not fall ~~to~~ [through] the basket. I am ~~shortest~~ [shorter] and ~~youngest~~ [younger] than Jeff, so I shoot more ~~slow~~ [slowly] and carefully. I take aim ~~confident~~ [confidently], ~~yet~~ [and] I find ~~exact~~ [exactly] the right angle. Then, I send the ball ~~for~~ [on] its way. When I make one basket ~~successful~~ [successfully], I begin to think about the next one, ~~but~~ [and] I picture myself ~~easy~~ [easily] winning a point.

ERRORS: PREPOSITIONS: 3; CONJUNCTIONS: 4;
COMPARATIVE/SUPERLATIVE ADJECTIVES: 3; ADVERBS: 9

124 Our Grandmother's House

My grandmother's house is the ~~old~~ [oldest] house ~~for~~ [in] town, ~~but~~ [and] it looms ~~ominous under~~ [ominously over] West Oak Street. It has the ~~taller~~ [tallest] tower ~~but~~ [and] the ~~steep~~ [steepest] roof I have ever seen. The children in the neighborhood ~~constant~~ [constantly] tell stories about it. They think that the house is haunted, but it is ~~actual surprising~~ [actually surprisingly] pleasant. ~~To~~ [On] hot summer days, the living room is my ~~favoritest~~ [favorite] place because it is ~~coolest~~ [cooler] than any other room. Heavy velvet drapes ~~efficient~~ [efficiently] keep the sun's heat out. In summer evenings, my brother ~~or~~ [and] I like to sit ~~from~~ [on] the wide front porch together and ~~slow~~ [slowly] sip lemonade.

ERRORS: PREPOSITIONS: 4; CONJUNCTIONS: 3;
COMPARATIVE/SUPERLATIVE ADJECTIVES: 5; ADVERBS: 6

Name: _____ Date: _____

My Cousin Jeff (123)

My cousin Jeff is oldest than I am, but he is taller too. He shoots baskets amazing good, but I still win many to our games. Jeff does not shoot as accurate as I do. He tosses the ball too quick. It hits the rim, but it does not fall to the basket. I am shortest and youngest than Jeff, so I shoot more slow and carefully. I take aim confident, yet I find exact the right angle. Then, I send the ball for its way. When I make one basket successful, I begin to think about the next one, but I picture myself easy winning a point.

✔ MIXED REVIEW

Name: _____ Date: _____

Our Grandmother's House (124)

My grandmother's house is the old house for town, but it looms ominous under West Oak Street. It has the taller tower but the steep roof I have ever seen. The children in the neighborhood constant tell stories about it. They think that the house is haunted, but it is actual surprising pleasant. To hot summer days, the living room is my favoritest place because it is coolest than any other room. Heavy velvet drapes efficient keep the sun's heat out. In summer evenings, my brother or I like to sit from the wide front porch together and slow sip lemonade.

✔ MIXED REVIEW

125 World Civilizations

There have ~~be~~ (been) many powerful civilizations in world history. Most of us ~~has readed~~ (have read)

about the Greeks, Romans, and Egyptians, but ~~us~~ (we) have not ~~herd~~ (heard) as much about other

important groups. For example, the Hittite ~~persons~~ (people) lived ~~to~~ (in) what ~~are~~ (is) now Turkey about

4,000 ~~year~~ (years) ago. The Hittites ~~was extreme~~ (were extremely) powerful ~~but~~ (and) inventive. ~~Them~~ (They) discovered how

to extract iron, ~~who~~ (which) they used ~~too~~ (to) make ~~strongest~~ (stronger) weapons. The Hittites also invented

steel, which is a building material made mostly of iron. They also developed ~~lightest,~~ (lighter,)

~~fastest~~ (faster) chariots. With ~~this,~~ (these,) the Hittites conquered many of ~~they~~ (their) neighbors.

> ✗ ERRORS: REGULAR PLURALS: 1; IRREGULAR PLURALS: 1; HOMOPHONES: 2; SUBJECT PRONOUNS: 2; POSSESSIVE PRONOUNS: 1; DEMONSTRATIVE PRONOUNS: 1; RELATIVE PRONOUNS: 1; PERFECT TENSE VERBS: 1; IRREGULAR LINKING VERBS: 1; SUBJECT/VERB AGREEMENT: 2; PREPOSITIONS: 1; CONJUNCTIONS: 1; ADJECTIVES: 3; ADVERBS: 1

126 A Rough Start

Today was Janelle's birthday party. The day started ~~bad,~~ (badly,) but ~~she~~ (it) ended ~~good.~~ (well.) First, I

~~forgetted~~ (forgot) to set the alarm, so I woke up a little ~~latest~~ (later) than usual. That would have ~~be~~ (been) fine.

I can dress ~~quick.~~ (quickly.) Unfortunately, that was not my only problem. I could not find Janelle's

gift. I ~~has wrap~~ (had wrapped) it and then ~~lain~~ (laid) it in the living room, but when I looked, I could not find

~~them everywhere.~~ (it anywhere.) Just then, my brother came downstairs and asked what was going on.

When ~~him~~ (he) heard what I was looking for, he laughed. He picked up ~~him~~ (his) jacket, ~~but~~ (and) the

present was underneath it. Mom ~~drived~~ (drove) me ~~for~~ (to) the party, and I was only five minutes late.

What started out as the ~~baddest~~ (worst) morning of the week became one of the ~~goodest~~ (best) ever!

> ✗ ERRORS: PRONOUN/NOUN AGREEMENT: 1; SUBJECT PRONOUNS: 1; POSSESSIVE PRONOUNS: 1; OBJECT PRONOUNS: 1; INDEFINITE PRONOUNS: 1; TRANSITIVE VERBS: 1; PERFECT TENSE VERBS: 1; IRREGULAR PAST TENSE VERBS: 2; IRREGULAR LINKING VERBS: 1; PREPOSITIONS: 1; CONJUNCTIONS: 1; ADJECTIVES: 3; ADVERBS: 3

130 DAILY EDITING • GRADE 5 • CD-104254 • © CARSON-DELLOSA

Name: _____ Date: _____

World Civilizations (125)

There have be many powerful civilizations in world history. Most of us has readed about the Greeks, Romans, and Egyptians, but us have not herd as much about other important groups. For example, the Hittite persons lived to what are now Turkey about 4,000 year ago. The Hittites was extreme powerful but inventive. Them discovered how to extract iron, who they used too make strongest weapons. The Hittites also invented steel, which is a building material made mostly of iron. They also developed lightest, fastest chariots. With this, the Hittites conquered many of they neighbors.

✔ CUMULATIVE REVIEW

Name: _____ Date: _____

A Rough Start (126)

Today was Janelle's birthday party. The day started bad, but she ended good. First, I forgetted to set the alarm, so I woke up a little latest than usual. That would have be fine. I can dress quick. Unfortunately, that was not my only problem. I could not find Janelle's gift. I has wrap it and then lain it in the living room, but when I looked, I could not find them everywhere. Just then, my brother came downstairs and asked what was going on. When him heard what I was looking for, he laughed. He picked up him jacket, but the present was underneath it. Mom drove me for the party, and I was only five minutes late. What started out as the baddest morning of the week became one of the goodest ever!

✔ CUMULATIVE REVIEW

127 My Travel Log

Yesterday after noon, I took the train to Eastland. My grand parents picked me up at the station. At first, I did not see them because the side walk out side the building was very crowded and every one was taller than I am. When ever I tried to look around, some one was in the way. There were two cow boys, some foot ball fans, and three ladies with big suit cases. Finally, I found my grand parents. They said that they had looked every where for me. They took me in side the rail road station for lunch. There is a great café near the news paper stand. Usually, what ever my grandfather orders is good. After lunch, Grandpa drove us out to their house. It is on a beach down the road from an old light house. No body operates it any more. Tomorrow, we will take a tour.

ERRORS: COMPOUND WORDS: 19

128 Recess Helpers

Some times, Jada and I stay in side to help Mrs. Jacobs and Ms. Hayden after lunch time. We are happy to do what ever they ask. On Tuesday, we cleaned out one of the cup boards in the class room. We recycled some old news papers, returned two basket balls to the supply room, and filed some home work papers in student folders. We finished quickly, and since there was no thing left to do, we joined the rest of the class out doors for recess. Every body was already playing, so we decided to watch one of the games. We stood on the side lines and cheered for which ever team made a point. We had fun, and no body was upset when the game ended in a tie.

ERRORS: COMPOUND WORDS: 15

Name: _____ Date: _____

My Travel Log (127)

Yesterday after noon, I took the train to Eastland. My grand parents picked me up at the station. At first, I did not see them because the side walk out side the building was very crowded and every one was taller than I am. When ever I tried to look around, some one was in the way. There were two cow boys, some foot ball fans, and three ladies with big suit cases. Finally, I found my grand parents. They said that they had looked every where for me. They took me in side the rail road station for lunch. There is a great café near the news paper stand. Usually, what ever my grandfather orders is good. After lunch, Grandpa drove us out to their house. It is on a beach down the road from an old light house. No body operates it any more. Tomorrow, we will take a tour.

✔ LOOK FOR: COMPOUND WORDS

Name: _____ Date: _____

Recess Helpers (128)

Some times, Jada and I stay in side to help Mrs. Jacobs and Ms. Hayden after lunch time. We are happy to do what ever they ask. On Tuesday, we cleaned out one of the cup boards in the class room. We recycled some old news papers, returned two basket balls to the supply room, and filed some home work papers in student folders. We finished quickly, and since there was no thing left to do, we joined the rest of the class out doors for recess. Every body was already playing, so we decided to watch one of the games. We stood on the side lines and cheered for which ever team made a point. We had fun, and no body was upset when the game ended in a tie.

✔ LOOK FOR: COMPOUND WORDS

Weather Report

Here   weather   February   fierce

~~Heer~~ is the ~~wether~~ report for today, ~~Febuary~~ 21. Last night, a ~~feirce~~ storm moved in from

tomorrow

the north. Strong winds will continue throughout most of today and ~~tomorow~~. We have

received   carefully

~~recieved~~ reports of fallen trees, so drive ~~carefuly~~. Skies will begin to clear sometime

Viewers   skiing

after two o'clock in the afternoon. ~~Veiwers~~ who enjoy ~~sking~~ will be happy to hear

that Misty Mountain Resort will open this weekend. The new practice slope is ready,

and children's lessons will be offered on Saturday and Sunday mornings. Rent your

skis   equipment   receive

~~skiis~~ and ~~equiptment~~ at the lodge or bring your own. Guests of the resort will ~~recieve~~

cocoa   restaurant

complimentary cups of hot ~~coco~~ at the lodge ~~resterant~~ when they check in. The staff

accommodate

will be happy to ~~acomodate~~ all of your needs.

❌ ERRORS: COMMONLY MISSPELLED WORDS: 15

 A Surprise Visit

March 8, 2010

Journal

Dear ~~Journel~~,

definitely   calendar

It has ~~definately~~ been a busy weekend. My ~~calender~~ was completely full. On Friday

friend

morning, I opened the door after the doorbell rang. I was expecting to see my ~~freind~~ and

neighbor   surprised

~~naybor~~, Adrienne. Instead, I saw Aunt Carol. I was happy and ~~suprised~~. There was not

much time to talk. I had to leave for school in a few minutes, and Mom would head to the

library

~~libary~~ in about an hour. "I took an early train," Aunt Carol explained. "I know everyone will

cupboards   vacuum

be gone all day. Don't worry about me. I will clean out the ~~cubords~~ and ~~vacume~~ the living

tonight   especially   privilege

room while you are gone. We will catch up ~~tonite~~. I ~~especialy~~ look forward to the ~~priviledge~~

of talking to you." Then, she gave me a big hug. We talked until Adrienne came.

❌ ERRORS: COMMONLY MISSPELLED WORDS: 12

Name: _____   Date: _____

Weather Report (129)

Heer is the wether report for today, Febuary 21. Last night, a feirce storm moved in from the north. Strong winds will continue throughout most of today and tomorow. We have recieved reports of fallen trees, so drive carefuly. Skies will begin to clear sometime after two o'clock in the afternoon. Veiwers who enjoy sking will be happy to hear that Misty Mountain Resort will open this weekend. The new practice slope is ready, and children's lessons will be offered on Saturday and Sunday mornings. Rent your skiis and equiptment at the lodge or bring your own. Guests of the resort will recieve complimentary cups of hot coco at the lodge resterant when they check in. The staff will be happy to acomodate all of your needs.

✔ LOOK FOR: SPELLING

Name: _____   Date: _____

A Surprise Visit (130)

March 8, 2010

Dear Journel,

It has definately been a busy weekend. My calender was completely full. On Friday morning, I opened the door after the doorbell rang. I was expecting to see my freind and naybor, Adrienne. Instead, I saw Aunt Carol. I was happy and suprised. There was not much time to talk. I had to leave for school in a few minutes, and Mom would head to the libary in about an hour. "I took an early train," Aunt Carol explained. "I know everyone will be gone all day. Don't worry about me. I will clean out the cubords and vacume the living room while you are gone. We will catch up tonite. I especialy look forward to the priviledge of talking to you." Then, she gave me a big hug. We talked until Adrienne came.

✔ LOOK FOR: SPELLING

131 Traffic Safety

Today, ~~Sergent~~ *Sergeant* Harold D. Chalmers visited our classroom. He arrived right on ~~scedule.~~ *schedule.*

He ~~reveiwed~~ *reviewed* traffic safety rules with us. He ~~brawt~~ *brought* a projector and showed us pictures

of the streets in our ~~nayborhood.~~ *neighborhood.* He said that people who walk are called *pedestrians.*

He told us that everyone on the road must follow rules. Sergeant Chalmers explained

that it is ~~especialy~~ *especially* important to use sidewalks and crosswalks. He also talked about

bicycle safety. He said that drivers are not ~~allways~~ *always* ~~consious~~ *conscious* of cyclists, so bike riders

must be ~~comitted~~ *committed* to watching out for cars. He also spoke about the importance of

being properly ~~equiped~~ *equipped* with helmets, mirrors, and knee and shoulder pads. After

Sergeant Chalmers left, we wrote letters thanking him for the ~~oportunity~~ *opportunity* to gain so

much ~~knowlege~~ *knowledge* about traffic safety.

 ERRORS: COMMONLY MISSPELLED WORDS: 12

132 Family History Homework

Our homework on Friday was to find out about our relatives. That afternoon, Mom was in

the backyard gardening. I told her about my assignment. She took me into the kichen

~~and sh~~owed me the family album. On the outside, it looked ~~ancent!~~ *ancient!* It was filled *kitchen* *ancient*

with ~~fasinating~~ *fascinating* pictures, letters, and newspaper ~~exerpts.~~ *excerpts.* There was a ~~senic~~ *scenic* picture of my

grandfather in a cowboy hat in front of a ~~gorgous~~ *gorgeous* mountain. There was also a picture of

my uncle in a train engineer's hat. He worked on a train. He wrote letters to his mom about

his travels. One of them was in a ~~seperate~~ *separate* album. There was a picture of my father when

he was a teenager too. He was at a ~~barbeque~~ *barbecue* on an ~~iland~~ *island* beach with his brothers. They

were all wearing ~~camoflage,~~ *camouflage,* and they were all about the same ~~hieght.~~ *height.* There was also a

~~souvenior~~ *souvenir* postcard from the trip. Mom ~~reccomended~~ *recommended* that I also talk to Grandma Jane.

 ERRORS: COMMONLY MISSPELLED WORDS: 13

Name: _____ Date: _____

Traffic Safety 131

Today, Sergent Harold D. Chalmers visited our classroom. He arrived right on scedule.

He reviewed traffic safety rules with us. He brawt a projector and showed us pictures

of the streets in our nayborhood. He said that people who walk are called *pedestrians*.

He told us that everyone on the road must follow rules. Sergeant Chalmers explained

that it is especialy important to use sidewalks and crosswalks. He also talked about

bicycle safety. He said that drivers are not allways consious of cyclists, so bike riders

must be comitted to watching out for cars. He also spoke about the importance of

being properly equiped with helmets, mirrors, and knee and shoulder pads. After

Sergeant Chalmers left, we wrote letters thanking him for the oportunity to gain so

much knowlege about traffic safety.

✔ LOOK FOR: SPELLING

- -

Name: _____ Date: _____

Family History Homework 132

Our homework on Friday was to find out about our relatives. That afternoon, Mom was in

the backyard gardening. I told her about my assignment. She took me into the kichen

and showed me the family album. On the outside, it looked ancent! It was filled

with fasinating pictures, letters, and newspaper exerpts. There was a senic picture of my

grandfather in a cowboy hat in front of a gorgous mountain. There was also a picture of

my uncle in a train engineer's hat. He worked on a train. He wrote letters to his mom about

his travels. One of them was in a seperate album. There was a picture of my father when

he was a teenager too. He was at a barbeque on an iland beach with his brothers. They

were all wearing camoflage, and they were all about the same hieght. There was also a

souvenier postcard from the trip. Mom reccomended that I also talk to Grandma Jane.

✔ LOOK FOR: SPELLING

133 Train Trip to the Mountains

Last week end, Grand pa took Jan and me to the mountains. He drove us to the

rail road station early on Saturday morning. While we waited for the train, he showed

us the route on a map. When the train arrived, we gathered our suit cases and ~~qwikly~~ *quickly*

walked out side. Then, we ~~climed~~ *climbed* aboard. After the conductor checked our tickets, we

moved to the dome car. We wanted to watch the ~~senery~~ *scenery* roll by. It was ~~fasinating~~ *fascinating* to see

the miles and miles of ~~paralel~~ *parallel* crop rows pass by my window. Every body in the car was

~~froindly~~. *friendly* By the time we arrived in the mountains that after noon, every one knew our

names. From now on, wherever I go, I want to take the train.

ERRORS: SPELLING: 14

134 Career Day

Last Friday was Career Day at our school. In the morning, speakers visited every

class room. In the afternoon, a program was ~~scoduled~~ *scheduled* in the auditorium. Every one

attended. The speakers included a news paper reporter, a rail road engineer, a real

cow boy, a basket ball player, and a ~~rostorant~~ *restaurant* manager. When ever a speaker asked

for questions, many ~~lisoners~~ *listeners* raised their hands. Our guests were happy to tell us

what ever we wanted to know. They were very flexible and ~~acomodating~~. *accommodating* At the end

of the day, a truck driver was describing his cross-country route. He told us about some

memorable trips in challenging ~~wether~~. *weather* Then, a ~~maintainance~~ *maintenance* worker told us about

fixing all kinds of things in apartment complexes. Suddenly, the bell rang. There was a

loud groan in the auditorium. Of course, no body wanted the event to end.

ERRORS: SPELLING: 15

Name: _____ Date: _____

Train Trip to the Mountains (133)

Last week end, Grand pa took Jan and me to the mountains. He drove us to the

rail road station early on Saturday morning. While we waited for the train, he showed

us the route on a map. When the train arrived, we gathered our suit cases and qwikly

walked out side. Then, we climed aboard. After the conductor checked our tickets, we

moved to the dome car. We wanted to watch the senery roll by. It was fasinating to see

the miles and miles of paralel crop rows pass by my window. Every body in the car was

freindly. By the time we arrived in the mountains that after noon, every one knew our

names. From now on, wherever I go, I want to take the train.

✔ MIXED REVIEW

Name: _____ Date: _____

Career Day (134)

Last Friday was Career Day at our school. In the morning, speakers visited every

class room. In the afternoon, a program was sceduled in the auditorium. Every one

attended. The speakers included a news paper reporter, a rail road engineer, a real

cow boy, a basket ball player, and a resterant manager. When ever a speaker asked

for questions, many liseners raised their hands. Our guests were happy to tell us

what ever we wanted to know. They were very flexible and acomodating. At the end

of the day, a truck driver was describing his cross-country route. He told us about some

memorable trips in challenging wether. Then, a maintainance worker told us about

fixing all kinds of things in apartment complexes. Suddenly, the bell rang. There was a

loud groan in the auditorium. Of course, no body wanted the event to end.

✔ MIXED REVIEW

135 — Our "New" School

The city ~~reemodeled~~ ^{remodeled} our school this summer. They held a ~~priview~~ ^{preview} night so that parents could see the school before it opened. Mom told me that they ~~ripainted~~ ^{repainted} the walls and ~~riplaced~~ ^{replaced} all of the ~~unncomfortable~~ ^{uncomfortable} chairs. They decided to ~~reeuse~~ ^{reuse} the tables. They just sanded them down and ~~rifinished~~ ^{refinished} them, but they look like new. They added two ~~Enternet~~ ^{Internet} connections and a new intercom speaker to each room. There are big, new ~~teluvisions~~ ^{televisions} too; our teachers like to ~~riplay~~ ^{replay} recordings of our plays and oral reports. The workmen also installed a new science lab for ~~enteractive~~ ^{interactive} assignments. It has five ~~mykroscopes~~ ^{microscopes}, a ~~teluscope~~ ^{telescope}, a weather station, and an experiment table with a big mirror. The mirror ~~riflects~~ ^{reflects} whatever the teacher is doing so that everybody can see.

I am really excited about school this year!

✗ ERRORS: WORDS WITH PREFIXES: 14

---

136 — Learning about the Lungs

Today, we learned about our lungs. First, our teacher explained that our lungs' job is to bring oxygen into our bodies and to carry away waste products from the air. She showed us ~~enternal~~ ^{internal} and ~~ixternal~~ ^{external} models of the body. She pointed to the lungs. Then, she ~~desappeared~~ ^{disappeared} into the closet for a minute and ~~reeappeared~~ ^{reappeared} with a box of tissues. She gave each of us one tissue. Then, she told us to ~~enhale~~ ^{inhale} and ~~ixhale~~ ^{exhale} while holding our tissues in front of us. Air is ~~envisible~~ ^{invisible}, but it made the tissues move. After the experiment, our teacher asked us to ~~ricall~~ ^{recall} what we had learned about the lungs. She ~~enncouraged~~ ^{encouraged} us to ~~reepeat~~ ^{repeat} what we had ~~discovered~~ ^{discovered} to our families at home. I was ~~desappointed~~ ^{disappointed} because I was ~~uhnable~~ ^{unable} to ~~reemember~~ ^{remember} very much, but I was able to show my little brother how to make the tissue move. He thought that it was very exciting.

✗ ERRORS: WORDS WITH PREFIXES: 14

Name: _____ Date: _____

Our "New" School 135

The city reemodeled our school this summer. They held a priview night so that parents

could see the school before it opened. Mom told me that they ripainted the walls

and riplaced all of the unncomfortable chairs. They decided to reeuse the tables.

They just sanded them down and rifinished them, but they look like new. They added

two Enternet connections and a new intercom speaker to each room. There are big,

new teluvisions too; our teachers like to riplay recordings of our plays and oral

reports. The workmen also installed a new science lab for enteractive assignments. It

has five mykroscopes, a teluscope, a weather station, and an experiment table with a

big mirror. The mirror riflects whatever the teacher is doing so that everybody can see.

I am really excited about school this year!

✔ LOOK FOR: WORDS WITH PREFIXES

Name: _____ Date: _____

Learning about the Lungs 136

Today, we learned about our lungs. First, our teacher explained that our lungs' job is

to bring oxygen into our bodies and to carry away waste products from the air. She

showed us enternal and ixternal models of the body. She pointed to the lungs. Then,

she desappeared into the closet for a minute and reeappeared with a box of tissues.

She gave each of us one tissue. Then, she told us to enhale and ixhale while holding our

tissues in front of us. Air is envisible, but it made the tissues move. After the experiment,

our teacher asked us to ricall what we had learned about the lungs. She enncouraged

us to reepeat what we had disscovered to our families at home. I was desappointed

because I was uhnable to reemember very much, but I was able to show my little

brother how to make the tissue move. He thought that it was very exciting.

✔ LOOK FOR: WORDS WITH PREFIXES

137 Sloppy Mistakes

I am ~~unnhappy~~ [unhappy] when I ~~uhncover~~ [uncover] ~~mosspelled~~ [misspelled] words in my homework assignments. It also makes me ~~uhncomfortable~~ [uncomfortable] to find ~~encomplete~~ [incomplete] sentences that I have ~~ovirlooked~~ [overlooked].

I know how it happens. Sometimes, I am doing my homework, and the ~~toluphone~~ [telephone] rings. I realize that I should not let it disturb me, but I cannot help it. I am ~~unnable~~ [unable] to resist! I answer it. My friends and I love to ~~rilive~~ [relive] the day together. After we talk, it is hard to ~~reoturn~~ [return] to work. I think that my homework is finished. ~~Unnfortunately~~ [Unfortunately], it is not. Sometimes, the teacher ~~riturns~~ [returns] it, and I have to ~~reowrite~~ [rewrite] the whole assignment. It is hard to ~~ovircome~~ [overcome] my disappointment and ~~rido~~ [redo] work that I have already done once.

ERRORS: WORDS WITH PREFIXES: 15

138 Kyle Saves the Submarine

Tonight, Channel 8 is going to ~~rirun~~ [rerun] an episode of my favorite ~~toluvision~~ [television] show. It is about a boy named Kyle who lives in a ~~subbdivision~~ [subdivision] near the beach. He has a ~~teluscope~~ [telescope] in his room. He uses it to watch ships at sea. One day, he spots a ~~sobmarine~~ [submarine]. He runs to tell his mom, but by the time he ~~reoturns~~ [returns], the boat has ~~desappeared~~ [disappeared]. Kyle watches the bay all afternoon, waiting for the sub to ~~riappear~~ [reappear]. His mother tries to interrupt him for dinner, but he remains at his post. It is very ~~unncomfortable~~ [uncomfortable] peering through that telescope, but he cannot leave the mystery ~~uhnsolved~~ [unsolved]. Finally, he is ~~unnable~~ [unable] to stay in that position any longer. He searches for news on the ~~Enternet~~ [Internet] and ~~unncovers~~ [uncovers] the information that a ~~suhbmarine~~ [submarine] is ~~overdue~~ [overdue] at the docks. He ~~enncourages~~ [encourages] his mom to call the Coast Guard. Thanks to him, rescuers are able to save the crew.

ERRORS: WORDS WITH PREFIXES: 16

Name: _____ Date: _____

Sloppy Mistakes 137

I am unnhappy when I uhncover messpelled words in my homework assignments. It also makes me uhncomfortable to find encomplete sentences that I have ovirlooked. I know how it happens. Sometimes, I am doing my homework, and the teluphone rings. I realize that I should not let it disturb me, but I cannot help it. I am unnable to resist! I answer it. My friends and I love to rilive the day together. After we talk, it is hard to reeturn to work. I think that my homework is finished. Unnfortunately, it is not. Sometimes, the teacher riturns it, and I have to reewrite the whole assignment. It is hard to ovircome my disappointment and rido work that I have already done once.

✔ LOOK FOR: WORDS WITH PREFIXES

Name: _____ Date: _____

Kyle Saves the Submarine 138

Tonight, Channel 8 is going to rirun an episode of my favorite teluvision show. It is about a boy named Kyle who lives in a subbdivision near the beach. He has a teluscope in his room. He uses it to watch ships at sea. One day, he spots a sobmarine. He runs to tell his mom, but by the time he reeturns, the boat has desappeared. Kyle watches the bay all afternoon, waiting for the sub to riappear. His mother tries to interrupt him for dinner, but he remains at his post. It is very unncomfortable peering through that telescope, but he cannot leave the mystery uhnsolved. Finally, he is unnable to stay in that position any longer. He searches for news on the Enternet and unncovers the information that a suhbmarine is ovardue at the docks. He enncourages his mom to call the Coast Guard. Thanks to him, rescuers are able to save the crew.

✔ LOOK FOR: WORDS WITH PREFIXES

(139) Reading about Real People and Science

Last month, our ~~assinment~~ [assignment] was to read a ~~biografy~~ [biography] or an ~~autobiografy~~ [autobiography]. I read about

Lance Armstrong. He is famous for winning ~~bicicle~~ [bicycle] races. Someday, I would like to

meet Mr. Armstrong. Perhaps he would give me his ~~autograf~~ [autograph]. Other students read

books about actors, governors, ~~geografers~~ [geographers], and philosophers. This month, we will

read books about science. I have checked out a book about ~~giology~~ [geology]. My uncle is

a ~~giologist~~ [geologist]. I am most interested in metamorphic and igneous rocks. The girl who sits

beside me is reading a book about ~~akwatic~~ [aquatic] animals. She visits the local ~~akwuarium~~ [aquarium]

every summer; she wants to be an ~~oceanografer~~ [oceanographer] someday.

✗ ERRORS: WORD ROOTS: 11

(140) Creative Homework Assignments

Mr. Murphy ~~assins~~ [assigns] homework every night. His ~~aktivities~~ [activities] are usually interesting. This

afternoon, he ~~assined~~ [assigned] ten ~~qwestions~~ [questions] about ~~geografy~~ [geography]. Last week, we made posters

about ~~recicling~~ [recycling] bottles and cans. We also wrote a ~~paragraf~~ [paragraph] about ~~microskopic~~ [microscopic]

aquatic life and a poem about metamorphosis. Next week, we will write journal

entries. We will also write ~~autobiografies~~ [autobiographies]. I do not think anybody will be interested in my

life. I am not an ~~aktor~~ [actor] or a sports star. Mr. Murphy says that does not matter. He thinks

that everyone is on a ~~qwest~~ [quest], like a hero in a movie. He wants us to think about what we

want in life. I have wanted a ~~telescop~~ [telescope] since I was three. Mr. Murphy says that could be

a part of my personal journey.

✗ ERRORS: WORD ROOTS: 12

Name: _____ Date: _____

Reading about Real People and Science (139)

Last month, our assinment was to read a biografy or an autobiografy. I read about Lance Armstrong. He is famous for winning bicicle races. Someday, I would like to meet Mr. Armstrong. Perhaps he would give me his autograf. Other students read books about actors, governors, geografers, and philosophers. This month, we will read books about science. I have checked out a book about giology. My uncle is a giologist. I am most interested in metamorphic and igneous rocks. The girl who sits beside me is reading a book about akwatic animals. She visits the local akwuarium every summer; she wants to be an oceanografer someday.

✓ LOOK FOR: WORD ROOTS

Name: _____ Date: _____

Creative Homework Assignments (140)

Mr. Murphy assins homework every night. His aktivities are usually interesting. This afternoon, he assined ten qwestions about geografy. Last week, we made posters about reciciling bottles and cans. We also wrote a paragraf about microskopic aquatic life and a poem about metamorphosis. Next week, we will write journal entries. We will also write autobiografies. I do not think anybody will be interested in my life. I am not an aktor or a sports star. Mr. Murphy says that does not matter. He thinks that everyone is on a qwest, like a hero in a movie. He wants us to think about what we want in life. I have wanted a telescop since I was three. Mr. Murphy says that could be a part of my personal journey.

✓ LOOK FOR: WORD ROOTS

141 Food Bank Dedication Speech

Ladies and gentlemen, I am proud to welcome you to this ~~historuc~~ event. We are *(historic)*

gathered to recognize the ~~bravist~~ and most ~~honorible~~ young man I have met in a long *(bravest)* *(honorable)*

time. Two years ago, he made it his ~~mishun~~ to buy ~~nutrityus~~ food for the ~~homeles~~ people *(mission)* *(nutritious)* *(homeless)*

of this city. His work started simply. First, he urged his parents to write letters to ~~governmunt~~ *(government)*

officials. Then, he wrote personal notes to small business ~~ownirs.~~ He told them about *(owners)*

hungry people he had met. He included the address and phone number of a local shelter

in each note. He invited the businesspeople to help if they could. His ~~hopefull,~~ ~~cheerfull,~~ *(hopeful)* *(cheerful)*

and ~~positave~~ attitude touched everyone he met. Thanks to him, more than 200 people no *(positive)*

longer feel the ~~torruble~~ ~~emptinuss~~ of hunger. The inspirational story of this young man has *(terrible)* *(emptiness)*

lead others to aid the ~~holpliss.~~ We are here to dedicate a new food bank in his honor. *(helpless)*

ERRORS: WORDS WITH SUFFIXES: 14

142 Be Friendly to Make Friends

Humans are social beings, and ~~lonolinuss~~ often leads to ~~unhappiniss.~~ It is ~~important~~ *(loneliness)* *(unhappiness)* *(important)*

for everyone to have ~~meaningfil~~ ~~relatianshops~~ with friends. If you are new to a school, *(meaningful)* *(relationships)*

try this ~~experimunt.~~ Develop a ~~positave~~ attitude. Assume that everyone in your class *(experiment)* *(positive)*

is interesting. Be ~~assertave~~ and take ~~acshion.~~ Say hello first. If the first person you *(assertive)* *(action)*

approach is not ~~friendlie,~~ do not take it ~~porsonilly.~~ His ~~roacshion~~ probably has nothing *(friendly)* *(personally)* *(reaction)*

to do with you. Just move on to someone else. Introduce yourself, and then ask

~~thoughtfull~~ questions. Listen ~~carefolly~~ to the answers. ~~Attentivenuss~~ is a rare quality, and *(thoughtful)* *(carefully)* *(Attentiveness)*

most people appreciate a good listener. Always remember, if you want to have good

friends, first you must be a good friend. This may sound difficult, but ~~friendshop~~ is a *(friendship)*

great treasure that is well worth the trouble.

ERRORS: WORDS WITH SUFFIXES: 16

Name: _____ Date: _____

Food Bank Dedication Speech 141

Ladies and gentlemen, I am proud to welcome you to this historuc event. We are

gathered to recognize the bravist and most honorible young man I have met in a long

time. Two years ago, he made it his mishun to buy nutrityus food for the homeles people

of this city. His work started simply. First, he urged his parents to write letters to governmunt

officials. Then, he wrote personal notes to small business ownirs. He told them about

hungry people he had met. He included the address and phone number of a local shelter

in each note. He invited the businesspeople to help if they could. His hopefull, cheerfull,

and positave attitude touched everyone he met. Thanks to him, more than 200 people no

longer feel the terruble emptinuss of hunger. The inspirational story of this young man has

lead others to aid the helpliss. We are here to dedicate a new food bank in his honor.

LOOK FOR: WORDS WITH SUFFIXES

Name: _____ Date: _____

Be Friendly to Make Friends 142

Humans are social beings, and lonelinuss often leads to unhappiniss. It is importent

for everyone to have meaningfil relatiansheps with friends. If you are new to a school,

try this experimunt. Develop a positave attitude. Assume that everyone in your class

is interesting. Be assertave and take acshion. Say hello first. If the first person you

approach is not friendlie, do not take it personilly. His reacshion probably has nothing

to do with you. Just move on to someone else. Introduce yourself, and then ask

thoughtfull questions. Listen carefelly to the answers. Attentivenuss is a rare quality, and

most people appreciate a good listener. Always remember, if you want to have good

friends, first you must be a good friend. This may sound difficult, but friendshep is a

great treasure that is well worth the trouble.

LOOK FOR: WORDS WITH SUFFIXES

SPELLING

143 A Positive Attitude

Kindness   learnable   experiment   cheerful   hopeful
~~Kindnus~~ is a ~~learnible~~ skill. Try this ~~experimunt~~: act ~~cheerfull~~ and ~~hopefol~~ for just one

carefully
hour. Listen to other people ~~carefuly~~ and consider what they have to say. If you do

joyful
not feel ~~joyfull~~, pretend that you are an actor in a film and smile anyway. Notice how

happiness
you feel at the end of the hour. Has your pretend ~~happinuss~~ become real? Now, try

fearful   hopeless   miserable
something else. Just for an hour, act ~~fearfull~~, sad, ~~hopelus~~, and ~~miserible~~. Notice how

loneliness   emptiness
you feel. Are you haunted by anger, ~~lonelinus~~, or ~~emptinus~~? Of course, you cannot

positive
choose how you feel, but you can choose how you act. Sometimes, a ~~positave~~

workable   contentment
attitude is a ~~workible~~ way to bring more ~~contentmunt~~ into your life.

ERRORS: WORDS WITH SUFFIXES: 16

144 Young Readers Book Fair

teacher   activity
Our ~~teachir~~, Mrs. Addison, has planned a special ~~activuty~~ for next week. She has

writer   reviewer   seller   librarian   readers
invited a ~~writer~~, a ~~reviewir~~, a book ~~sellir~~, and a ~~librariun~~ to our young ~~readirs~~ book fair.

dramatic   exciting
They will tell us about the funniest, most ~~dramatue~~, and most ~~exciteng~~ books for fifth

graders   energetic   author   actor   singer
~~gradirs~~. Then, Lawrence Lamonte, an ~~energetue~~ ~~auther~~, ~~acter~~, and ~~singir~~, will teach us

comedic   latest   careful
some ~~comedee~~ songs from his ~~latist~~ book. Mrs. Addison wants us to take ~~carefull~~ notes.

thoughtful
After the fair, we will write ~~thoughtfull~~ thank-you letters to all of our guests.

ERRORS: WORDS WITH SUFFIXES: 18

Name: _____ Date: _____

A Positive Attitude 143

Kindnus is a learnible skill. Try this experimunt: act cheerfull and hopefol for just one hour. Listen to other people carefuly and consider what they have to say. If you do not feel joyfull, pretend that you are an actor in a film and smile anyway. Notice how you feel at the end of the hour. Has your pretend happinuss become real? Now, try something else. Just for an hour, act fearfull, sad, hopelus, and miserible. Notice how you feel. Are you haunted by anger, lonelinus, or emptinus? Of course, you cannot choose how you feel, but you can choose how you act. Sometimes, a positave attitude is a workible way to bring more contentmunt into your life.

✔ LOOK FOR: WORDS WITH SUFFIXES

Name: _____ Date: _____

Young Readers Book Fair 144

Our teachir, Mrs. Addison, has planned a special activuty for next week. She has invited a writor, a reviewir, a book sellir, and a librariun to our young readirs book fair. They will tell us about the funniest, most dramatuc, and most exciteng books for fifth gradirs. Then, Lawrence Lamonte, an energetuc auther, acter, and singir, will teach us some comedec songs from his latist book. Mrs. Addison wants us to take carefull notes. After the fair, we will write thoughtfull thank-you letters to all of our guests.

✔ LOOK FOR: WORDS WITH SUFFIXES

145 Ashley's New Friend

Ashley's family moved into a new ~~sobdivision~~ [subdivision] in June. Their first night, there was an ~~energetuc~~ [energetic] knock at the door. It was the girl next door. ~~Cheerfily,~~ [Cheerfully] she introduced herself. Her name was Barbara. Her father was a biology ~~researchir~~ [researcher] at the ~~universoty,~~ [university] and her mother was a science ~~teachor.~~ [teacher] Barbara explained that her hobby was science. She invited Ashley to her house. She had a ~~powerfull~~ [powerful] ~~microscop~~ [microscope] and a real ~~stethoskop.~~ [stethoscope] There was an excellent view of Mars, so Barbara led Ashley into her backyard where her family's ~~teleskope~~ [telescope] was set up. The girls examined several objects in the night sky. Ashley was excited. She had never looked through a real ~~telloscope~~ [telescope] before. When Barbara asked to meet the next morning to gather pond water so that they could look at ~~microskopic~~ [microscopic] ~~akwatic~~ [aquatic] life under her ~~mikroscope,~~ [microscope] Ashley knew it was going to be a ~~wonderfull~~ [wonderful] summer.

✗ ERRORS: SPELLING: 16

---

146 Antonyms

Today in class, we completed an ~~aktivity~~ [activity] on antonyms. The word *~~happinus~~* [happiness] is an antonym of the word *unhappiness*. Antonyms are opposites. Not all words have antonyms, but many words do. Here are some other examples. If someone is ~~unlikible,~~ [unlikable] that person is not ~~likuble.~~ [likable] If a girl is ~~hopefull,~~ [hopeful] she is not ~~hopeluss.~~ [hopeless] If your little brother is ~~carefull,~~ [careful] he is not ~~caroluss.~~ [careless] If a boy is ~~miserible,~~ [miserable] he certainly is not ~~cheerfol.~~ [cheerful] If a door is ~~unnlocked,~~ [unlocked] it is not locked. If rules are ~~uhnfair,~~ [unfair] they are not fair. *~~Smoothnuss~~* [Smoothness] is the opposite of *~~roughniss,~~* [roughness] and *~~calmnuss~~* [calmness] is the opposite of *~~excitemunt.~~* [excitement] A ~~qwestion~~ [question] is the opposite of an answer because an answer is the solution or response to the problem. Antonyms are another way to help you clarify a word's ~~definishon.~~ [definition] Our ~~assinment~~ [assignment] is to write a list of 10 more antonym pairs.

✗ ERRORS: SPELLING: 19

Name: _____ Date: _____

Ashley's New Friend　(145)

Ashley's family moved into a new sobdivision in June. Their first night, there was an energetuc knock at the door. It was the girl next door. Cheerfily, she introduced herself. Her name was Barbara. Her father was a biology researchir at the universety, and her mother was a science teachor. Barbara explained that her hobby was science. She invited Ashley to her house. She had a powerfull microscop and a real stethoskop. There was an excellent view of Mars, so Barbara led Ashley into her backyard where her family's teleskope was set up. The girls examined several objects in the night sky. Ashley was excited. She had never looked through a real tellescope before. When Barbara asked to meet the next morning to gather pond water so that they could look at microskopic akwatic life under her mikroscope, Ashley knew it was going to be a wonderfull summer.

✔ MIXED REVIEW

Name: _____ Date: _____

Antonyms　(146)

Today in class, we completed an aktivity on antonyms. The word *happinus* is an antonym of the word *unhappiness*. Antonyms are opposites. Not all words have antonyms, but many words do. Here are some other examples. If someone is unlikible, that person is not likuble. If a girl is hopefull, she is not hopeluss. If your little brother is carefull, he is not careluss. If a boy is miserible, he certainly is not cheerfel. If a door is unnlocked, it is not locked. If rules are uhnfair, they are not fair. *Smoothnuss* is the opposite of *roughniss,* and *calmnuss* is the opposite of *excitemunt.* A qwestion is the opposite of an answer because an answer is the solution or response to the problem. Antonyms are another way to help you clarify a word's definishon. Our assinment is to write a list of 10 more antonym pairs.

✔ MIXED REVIEW

147

Art Exhibit Preview

To: jeremy@nomail.zap
From: ivan@nomail.zap

Dear Jeremy,

This morning, my dad took me to the ~~universety~~ *university*. We were invited to ~~preeview~~ *preview* an art exhibition. We arrived on ~~scedule~~ *schedule*, and ~~Professer~~ *Professor* Mann greeted us. He is a ~~risearcher~~ *researcher* in the ~~giology~~ *geology* ~~departmunt~~ *department* and a ~~freind~~ *friend* of my father's. I was ~~empressed~~ *impressed* by his ~~kindnuss~~ *kindness* and ~~thoughtfulnis~~ *thoughtfulness*. He walked ~~thru~~ *through* the gallery with us. It was ~~wonderfell~~ *wonderful*. Most of the paintings were ~~gorgous~~ *gorgeous*, although there were a few that I did not under⌣stand. What are you doing this wee⌣k end? ~~Woud~~ *Would* you like to go to the museum with us?

Your friend,
Ivan

✗ ERRORS: SPELLING: 17

 148

Writing Rough Drafts

Today, our home⌣work ~~assinment~~ *assignment* was to write a ~~paragraf~~ *paragraph* about a favorite ~~aktivity~~ *activity*. Mr. Greg ~~incouraged~~ *encouraged* us to begin with a ~~qwik~~ *quick* first draft. He explained that it was OK to be ~~careluss~~ *careless* and make mistakes in the first version. I wrote my paragraph, and it was ~~terruble~~ *terrible*. ~~Fortunatelly~~ *Fortunately*, I had plenty of time to ~~ripair~~ *repair* the problems before ~~sobmitting~~ *submitting* my paper. I made the ~~alteratians~~ *alterations* in red pencil, and then I ~~reewrote~~ *rewrote* the whole paragraph on another sheet of paper. I am extremely proud of the ~~risult~~ *result*. Next month, my ~~reeport~~ *report* about our town's ~~historue~~ *historic* buildings is due. I was afraid to begin writing because I ~~thout~~ *thought* my work had to be perfect the first time. Now, I am ~~definately~~ *definitely* confident that I can do a good job.

✗ ERRORS: SPELLING: 18

Name: _____ Date: _____

Art Exhibit Preview (147)

To: jeremy@nomail.zap
From: ivan@nomail.zap

Dear Jeremy,

This morning, my dad took me to the universety. We were invited to preeview an art exhibition. We arrived on scedule, and Professer Mann greeted us. He is a risearcher in the giology departmunt and a freind of my father's. I was empressed by his kindnuss and thoughtfulnis. He walked thru the gallery with us. It was wonderfell. Most of the paintings were gorgous, although there were a few that I did not under stand. What are you doing this week end? Woud you like to go to the museum with us?

Your friend,
Ivan

✔ CUMULATIVE REVIEW

Name: _____ Date: _____

Writing Rough Drafts (148)

Today, our home work assinment was to write a paragraf about a favorite aktivity. Mr. Greg incouraged us to begin with a qwik first draft. He explained that it was OK to be careluss and make mistakes in the first version. I wrote my paragraph, and it was terruble. Fortunatelly, I had plenty of time to ripair the problems before sobmitting my paper. I made the alteratians in red pencil, and then I reewrote the whole paragraph on another sheet of paper. I am extremely proud of the risult. Next month, my reeport about our town's historuc buildings is due. I was afraid to begin writing because I thout my work had to be perfect the first time. Now, I am definately confident that I can do a good job.

✔ CUMULATIVE REVIEW

149 Llamas and Alpacas

Llamas and alpacas are ~~are~~ domesticated members of ^the^ camel family. Both ~~of~~ llamas and

alpacas live in South America. They ~~is~~ are relatives of wild guanacos and vicunas. Alpacas ^are^

raised in ^the^ mountains of Peru and Bolivia. They have thick ~~thick~~ coats, which herders shear

once ^a^ year. Finer ~~finest~~ than sheep's wool, alpaca fur is ~~weaved~~ woven into beautiful,

warm cloth. Larger ^and^ sturdier than alpacas, llamas ^were^ used as pack animals long before the

arrival of the Spanish in South America. Well-suited to ~~of~~ the climate of the Andes, llamas

can ~~could~~ survive without ~~with out~~ drinking water for long periods. The water they ~~them~~

need is supplied by the green plants they eat. Like their ~~they're~~ distant relatives in the

Middle East, llamas and alpacas have served people ~~persons~~ for many generations.

ERRORS: DELETE EXTRA WORDS: 13; INSERT MISSING WORDS: 6

150 Cats

Cats have been favorite pets ^for^ thousands of years. They were ~~was~~ important to ~~old~~

ancient Egyptians, protecting their ~~there~~ supplies of grain from hungry ~~mouses~~ mice ^and^

rats. Paintings and sculptures reveal ~~what~~ that the Egyptian goddess of love, Bast,

had ^the^ head of ^a^ cat. In the 21st century, cats are no ~~not~~ longer worshipped, but ~~them~~

they are still very ~~very~~ important to millions of ~~from~~ devoted pet owners around ~~about~~

the world. Artists have ~~paint~~ painted them. Poets have written about them. Films ^have^

been ~~maked~~ made ^about^ them. Cats add beauty, grace, and affection to many homes.

ERRORS: DELETE EXTRA WORDS: 12; INSERT MISSING WORDS: 6

Name: _____ Date: _____

Llamas and Alpacas (149)

Llamas and alpacas are are domesticated members of camel family. Both of llamas and alpacas live in South America. They is are relatives of wild guanacos and vicunas. Alpacas raised in mountains of Peru and Bolivia. They have thick thick coats, which herders shear once year. Finer finest than sheep's wool, alpaca fur is weaved woven into beautiful, warm cloth. Larger sturdier than alpacas, llamas used as pack animals long before the arrival of the Spanish in South America. Well-suited to of the climate of the Andes, llamas can could survive without with out drinking water for long periods. The water they them need is supplied by the green plants they eat. Like their they're distant relatives in the Middle East, llamas and alpacas have served people persons for many generations.

✔ LOOK FOR: EXTRA OR MISSING WORDS

Name: _____ Date: _____

Cats (150)

Cats have been favorite pets thousands of years. They were was important to old ancient Egyptians, protecting their there supplies of grain from hungry mouses mice rats. Paintings and sculptures reveal what that the Egyptian goddess of love, Bast, had head of cat. In the 21st century, cats are no not longer worshipped, but them they are still very very important to millions of from devoted pet owners around about the world. Artists have paint painted them. Poets have written about them. Films been maked made them. Cats add beauty, grace, and affection to many homes.

✔ LOOK FOR: EXTRA OR MISSING WORDS

151 My Favorite Person

Danny McDonald
March 21, 2010

My older old brother, Martin, is my favorite person. He is not no perfect. In fact, he is as clumsy clumsier as a bull in a china shop. Whenever whichever he walks into of a room, something break breaks. Martin he broke my me goldfish bowl twice; he saved the fish both times. It is not his fault that he him breaks things. He is already big, and he is still growing. I love Martin because he is gentle and kind. He listens to me, and he protects me. He may be awkward, but he is the goodest best brother in the world.

ERRORS: DELETE EXTRA WORDS: 10; INSERT MISSING WORDS: 9

152 Winter Festival Parade

Kimberley wanted to be in of the Winter Festival parade. She saw seen a poster to about an art contest. The winner of that these contest would ride on the Main Street Art Shop's Shops float in the parade. Kimberley knew she was a good artist. She spent spended all of her allowance on poster board, paint, and other supplies. When her friend Tessa asked she her to ride on the the plumbing service's float, Kimberley said no. Kimberley's mom shook her head. "Don't put all of your eggs in one basket," she warn warned. Kimberley would not listen. She was were sure she would win the contest. Kimberley could not never believe it when Jaime Flores won. She had have to watch the parade from to the sidewalk.

ERRORS: DELETE EXTRA WORDS: 13; INSERT MISSING WORDS: 6

Name: _____ Date: _____

My Favorite Person **151**

Danny McDonald
March 21, 2010

My older old brother, Martin, my favorite person. He is not no perfect. In fact, he is as

clumsy clumsier as a bull a china shop. Whenever whichever he walks into of a room,

something break breaks. Martin he broke my me goldfish bowl twice; he saved the fish

both times. It not his fault that he him breaks things. He already big, he is still growing.

I love Martin because he is gentle kind. He listens to me, he protects me. He may be

awkward, but he the goodest best brother the world.

✔ LOOK FOR: EXTRA OR MISSING WORDS

Name: _____ Date: _____

Winter Festival Parade **152**

Kimberley wanted to be in of the Winter Festival parade. She saw seen a poster to

about an art contest. The winner of that these contest would ride on the Main Street

Art Shop's Shops float in the parade. Kimberley knew she a good artist. She spent

spended all of her allowance on poster board, paint, other supplies. When her friend

Tessa asked she her to ride on the the plumbing service's float, Kimberley said no.

Kimberley's mom shook head. "Don't put all of your eggs one basket," she warn

warned. Kimberley not listen. She was were sure she would win contest. Kimberley

could not never believe it when Jaime Flores won. She had have to watch the parade

from to the sidewalk.

✔ LOOK FOR: EXTRA OR MISSING WORDS

153 Nature Walk

Our science club will host a (walk/nature) on Saturday afternoon. At first, we thought it would be a (idea/good) to eat (the/in) park. Then, we talked about it (decided/and) to go after lunch instead. We will meet (front/in) of the school (two/at) o'clock. Bring (bottle/a) of water and a (bag/plastic) filled with trail mix. There is (recipe/a) on the back of (paper/this). Please do not (peanuts/include). Some people are extremely allergic (them/to). We only have (vans/three). If your mother or father (like/would) to drive, that would (great/be).

✗ ERRORS: TRANSPOSE WORDS: 15 PAIRS

154 Camping Journal

May 18, 2011

Dear Journal,

Although I thought I would not (camping/like), I must admit that I was wrong. I (not/did) know how (fun/much) it could be. Last night, my (took/family) a star walk. In the mountains, (stars/the) are quite (sight/a). I (not/could) believe (bright/how) they were. My (brought/brother) his lighted star map. He (been/has) taking an astronomy class. He talked about (constellation/each). After (walk/our), Dad built a campfire, and Mom made hot chocolate. We (planning/are) to take a (hike/wildlife) with the park ranger later (morning/this). I wonder what we will see.

✗ ERRORS: TRANSPOSE WORDS: 15 PAIRS

Name: _____ Date: _____

Nature Walk 153

Our science club will host a walk nature on Saturday afternoon. At first, we thought it would be a idea good to eat the in park. Then, we talked about it decided and to go after lunch instead. We will meet front in of the school two at o'clock. Bring bottle a of water and a bag plastic filled with trail mix. There is recipe a on the back of paper this. Please do not peanuts include. Some people are extremely allergic them to. We only have vans three. If your mother or father like would to drive, that would great be!

✔ LOOK FOR: WORD ORDER

Name: _____ Date: _____

Camping Journal 154

May 18, 2011

Dear Journal,

Although I thought I would not camping like, I must admit that I was wrong. I not did know how fun much it could be. Last night, my took family a star walk. In the mountains, stars the are quite sight a. I not could believe bright how they were. My brought brother his lighted star map. He been has taking an astronomy class. He talked about constellation each. After walk our, Dad built a campfire, and Mom made hot chocolate. We planning are to take a hike wildlife with the park ranger later morning this. I wonder what we will see.

✔ LOOK FOR: WORD ORDER

A Sweater from Nona

To: nona@nomail.zap
From: ruby@nomail.zap

Dear Aunt Nona,

I am finally writing (thank)(to)you for the sweater you knitted (me)(for). When the delivery man knocked on our door, (knew)(I)it was a package from you. What a (design)(beautiful)! You have a knack for knowing just what (need)(I). I will knit a scarf to go with it. I cannot (it)(do)right now though. I hurt (wrist)(my)and my thumb. Yesterday, my whole hand (numb)(was). Uncle George (us)(took)on a (ride)(sleigh)through the woods. A (tree)(low)limb hit (hand)(my). Do (worry)(not). It is (better)(much)today. Thanks again (the)(for)sweater!

Your niece,
Ruby

ERRORS: TRANSPOSE WORDS: 15 PAIRS

A Perfect Afternoon

Today, Dad and I took (walk)(a)through the forest near the (cabin)(mountain). Every (bough)(pine)was covered (snow)(with). Every (limb)(maple)was covered too. It was (still)(absolutely). We (not)(did)want to talk. Somehow, it seemed wrong to break (silence)(the). We were standing by a (pond)(frozen), the wind started to blow. The cold (through)(cut)my jacket like a knife. Even (nose)(my)and ears were numb. Suddenly, we heard a (neigh)(familiar). Mr. Zane's horse trotted up to us pulling a sleigh. Mr. Zane invited us to (in)(climb). He handed me a (blanket)(warm), and away we went. For dinner, Mom made (chicken)(fried)with roasted potatoes and corn. What a (ending)(delicious)for a perfect afternoon!

ERRORS: TRANSPOSE WORDS: 16 PAIRS

Name: _____ Date: _____

A Sweater from Nona (155)

To: nona@nomail.zap
From: ruby@nomail.zap

Dear Aunt Nona,

I am finally writing thank to you for the sweater you knitted me for. When the delivery man knocked on our door, knew I it was a package from you. What a design beautiful! You have a knack for knowing just what need I! I will knit a scarf to go with it. I cannot it do right now though. I hurt wrist my and my thumb. Yesterday, my whole hand numb was. Uncle George us took on a ride sleigh through the woods. A tree low limb hit hand my. Do worry not. It is better much today. Thanks again the for sweater!

Your niece,
Ruby

LOOK FOR: WORD ORDER

Name: _____ Date: _____

A Perfect Afternoon (156)

Today, Dad and I took walk a through the forest near the cabin mountain. Every bough pine was covered snow with. Every limb maple was covered too. It was still absolutely. We not did want to talk. Somehow, it seemed wrong to break silence the. We were standing by a pond frozen; the wind started to blow. The cold through cut my jacket like a knife. Even nose my and ears were numb. Suddenly, we heard a neigh familiar. Mr. Zane's horse trotted up to us pulling a sleigh. Mr. Zane invited us to in climb. He handed me a blanket warm, and away we went. For dinner, Mom made chicken fried with roasted potatoes and corn. What a ending delicious for a perfect afternoon!

LOOK FOR: WORD ORDER

Camping Adventures

Every summer, thousands of families (camping go). Some have ~~has~~ special recreational vehicles equipped (stoves with), refrigerators, (even and) television sets. Others have (backpacks simple), sleeping bags, and tents. All enjoy ~~enjoys~~ spending time together outdoors. Many daytime activities (available are) to campers, including hiking, rock climbing, rafting, swimming, fishing, wildlife watching, and photography. Evening pleasures include ~~includes~~ singing songs around the campfire and stargazing. Wherever ~~where ever~~ campers go and however they ~~he~~ spend (time their), they return home with tales ~~tails~~ about their adventures.

ERRORS: DELETE EXTRA WORDS: 7; INSERT MISSING WORDS: 2; TRANSPOSE WORDS: 6 PAIRS

Pipefish

Pipefish are tube-shaped relatives of the sea horse. They ~~has~~ have (snouts long), small mouths, and no ~~teeths~~ teeth. They eat (creatures tiny) called *crustaceans*. Most live in warm seas, though some thrive in freshwater. There are more ~~most~~ than 100 different species, or types, of pipefish. Some are as long as ~~you~~ your forearm. Others are ~~more~~ smaller than your (finger little). All have an (skin armor-like) composed of bony plates. Usually brown, olive-colored, or green, they are difficult to spot in the water. Like sea horses, male pipefish care for their ~~there~~ mates' eggs. The female ~~place~~ places (eggs the) in a pouch on her mate's abdomen. The baby pipefish hatch there. They stay until they are ready to take care of themselves. The whole process usually takes about two weeks.

ERRORS: DELETE EXTRA WORDS: 7; INSERT MISSING WORDS: 3; TRANSPOSE WORDS: 5 PAIRS

Name: _____ Date: _____

Camping Adventures (157)

Every summer, thousands of families camping go. Some have has special recreational vehicles equipped stoves with, refrigerators, even and television sets. Others have backpacks simple, sleeping bags, tents. All enjoy enjoys spending time together outdoors. Many daytime activities available are to campers, including hiking, rock climbing, rafting, swimming, fishing, wildlife watching, and photography. Evening pleasures include includes singing songs the campfire and stargazing. Wherever where ever campers go and however they he spend time their, they return home with tales tails about their adventures.

✔ CUMULATIVE REVIEW

Name: _____ Date: _____

Pipefish (158)

Pipefish tube-shaped relatives of the sea horse. They has have snouts long, small mouths, and no tooths teeth. They eat creatures tiny called *crustaceans*. Most live warm seas, though some thrive in freshwater. There are more most than 100 different species, or types, of pipefish. Some are as long as you your forearm. Others are more smaller than your finger little. All have an skin armor-like composed of bony plates. Usually brown, olive-colored, green, they are difficult to spot in the water. Like sea horses, male pipefish care for their there mates' eggs. The female place places eggs the in a pouch on her mate's abdomen. The baby pipefish hatch there. They stay until they are ready to take care of themselves. The whole process usually takes about two weeks.

✔ CUMULATIVE REVIEW

159 The Railway Train

My ~~most~~ favorite poem about (trains) is by Emily Dickinson. It called "The Railway Train." In the first line, "I like to see it lap the miles," Dickinson suggests that a train is like an animal drinking. In the second line, the poet continues ~~his~~ her animal theme. The engine ~~take~~ takes time to "lick valleys up" and "feed itself at tanks." In the last line of the first stanza, the train creature ~~stop~~ stops eating and drinking. She uses the word "prodigious" (almost superhuman) to describe the way it steps around an entire mountain range. In the last stanza, we ~~discovers~~ discover that the animal is a horse, it neighs and stops at "its own stable door." The entire poem is a clever play on words because, in the 1800s, the steam locomotive was known as an "iron horse."

> **ERRORS: SEMICOLONS: 1; COMMAS: 1; QUOTATION MARKS: 4; PARENTHESES: 1; PRONOUN/NOUN AGREEMENT: 1; SUBJECT/VERB AGREEMENT: 3; DELETE EXTRA WORDS: 1; INSERT MISSING WORDS: 4; TRANSPOSE WORDS: 1 PAIR**

160 Springtime Poem

Spring is a time of new beginnings, many authors have celebrated it. The british poet William blake opens ~~he~~ his poem "Spring" with this exclamation: "Sound the flute!" He continues with "Now it's mute." The end of the first stanza celebrates the (that fact) nightingales sing ~~continual~~ continually in the spring. ~~This~~ These small singers are ~~unnlike~~ unlike the flutes mentioned in the first lines, ~~who~~ which play for a while and then ~~stops.~~ stop. In the stanza's final line, Blake uses the adverb *merrily* twice. The three-syllable word's lilting sound adds music to the poem and ~~suggest~~ suggests the ~~repetitus~~ repetitious song of a bird.

> **ERRORS: MAKE UPPERCASE: 2; SEMICOLONS: 1; APOSTROPHES: 2; QUOTATION MARKS: 2; EXCLAMATION POINTS: 1; POSSESSIVE PRONOUNS: 1; DEMONSTRATIVE PRONOUNS: 1; RELATIVE PRONOUNS: 1; SUBJECT/VERB AGREEMENT: 2; ADVERBS: 1; SPELLING: 2; TRANSPOSE WORDS: 1 PAIR**

Name: _____ Date: _____

The Railway Train 159

My most favorite poem about train a is by Emily Dickinson. It called The Railway Train." In the first line, I like to see it lap the miles," Dickinson suggests that a train is like an animal drinking. In second line, the poet continues his animal theme. The engine take time to "lick valleys up" and "feed itself at tanks. In the last line the first stanza the train creature stop eating and drinking. She uses the word "prodigious" almost superhuman) to describe the way it steps around an entire mountain range. In the last stanza, we discovers that animal is a horse it neighs and stops at "its own stable door. The entire poem is a clever play on words because, in the 1800s, the steam locomotive was known as an "iron horse."

✔ FINAL REVIEW

Name: _____ Date: _____

Springtime Poem 160

Spring is a time of new beginnings many authors have celebrated it. The british poet William blake opens he poem "Spring with this exclamation: "Sound the flute." He continues with "Now it's mute. The end of the first stanza celebrates the that fact nightingales sing continual in the spring. This small singers are unnlike the flutes mentioned in the first lines, who play for a while and then stops. In the stanzas final line, Blake uses the adverb *merrily* twice. The three-syllable words lilting sound adds music to the poem and suggest the repetitus song of a bird.

✔ FINAL REVIEW

Science Fair

Mrs. Kennedy's class is planning a science fair. One-half of the class will work on

life science projects, and the other half will work on physical science projects. The

students is working—for the next two week anyway, in small groups. The groups'
(are) *(weeks)*

projects—whether charts, pictures, models, or reports are extreme exciting. Mariah's
(extremely)

group is keeping a weather chart. The girls' chart will stay on the bulletin board all

year. The following three boys are working together, Miguel, Julio, and Hector. They

are modeling distances the in solar system. The boys' planet models will hang on the

cafeteria wall during the science fair.

> ✗ ERRORS: COLONS: 1; HYPHENS: 1; COMMAS: 3; APOSTROPHES: 4; DASHES: 2;
> PLURALS: 1; SUBJECT/VERB AGREEMENT: 1; ADVERBS: 1; TRANSPOSE WORDS: 1 PAIR

Studying Ecosystems

Mr. Manzell's class are studying ecosystems (systems made up of ecological
(is)

communities of living things interacting with their environment) His students has select
(have selected)

partners. Each pair have wrote 10 questions—no more, no less, to answer. Pat and
(has written)

Heather are using the library. The girls' job has be more easier since Ms. McIntosh (the
(been)

librarian) showed they how to use the card catalog. Lamar and Jeremy are searching
(them)

the Internet. The boys' pictures have already filled bulletin board next to the computer.
(the)

On Monday (the day before a an class trip to the nature center), the students will share

there questions answers with the class.
(their) *(and)*

> ✗ ERRORS: APOSTROPHES: 3; PARENTHESES: 3; DASHES: 1; HOMOPHONES: 1;
> OBJECT PRONOUNS: 1; PERFECT TENSE VERBS: 2; IRREGULAR LINKING VERBS: 1;
> SUBJECT/VERB AGREEMENT: 1; DELETE EXTRA WORDS: 2; INSERT MISSING WORDS: 2

Name: _____ Date: _____

Science Fair (161)

Mrs. Kennedy's class is planning a science fair. One half of the class will work on life science projects, and the other half will work on physical science projects. The students is working—for the next two week anyway in small groups. The groups projects—whether charts pictures models or reports are extreme exciting. Mariahs group is keeping a weather chart. The girls chart will stay on the bulletin board all year. The following three boys are working together Miguel, Julio, and Hector. They are modeling distances the in solar system. The boys planet models will hang on the cafeteria wall during the science fair.

Name: _____ Date: _____

Studying Ecosystems (162)

Mr. Manzells class are studying ecosystems (systems made up of ecological communities of living things interacting with their environment. His students has select partners. Each pair have wrote 10 questions—no more, no less to answer. Pat and Heather are using the library. The girls job has be more easier since Ms. McIntosh (the librarian showed they how to use the card catalog. Lamar and Jeremy are searching the Internet. The boys pictures have already filled bulletin board next to the computer. On Monday the day before a an class trip to the nature center), the students will share there questions answers with the class.

163 **Poetry Book Report**

The Kingfisher Book of Children's Poetry is an anthology (a collection of literary pieces). The poems were chosen by Michael Rosen, a british poet which nose how to make [who knows] poetry fun for children. Their are many great poems in this book. [There] The ones I likes best [like] are the following "Greedy Dog" by James Hurley, "Waking Up" by Eleanor Farjeon, "I'm Nobody" buy Emily Dickinson and "The Honey Pot" by Alan Riddell. Some of Michael [by] Rosen's poems in the book too. I like they very much. [are] [them]

 164 **Handmade Birthday Cards**

Would you like to make you own birth day cards? It is easy to do, and persons will [your] [people] love your one-of-a-kind work of art First, you will need a sheet of heavy paper. Fold it in half. Then decorates the front panel with a design, a drawing or a photograf. You [decorate] [photograph] can use markers, paint or pencils. If you use crayons press light because heavy wax [lightly] layers smear easy. After you finish the cover design, open your card, careful print a [easily] [carefully] short message, sign your name. What a great way to celebrate a family member's [and] special day? Oh, and don't forget to sing "Happy Birthday!" [!]

Name: _____ Date: _____

Poetry Book Report (163)

The Kingfisher Book of Childrens Poetry is an anthology a collection of literary pieces).
The poems were chosen by Michael Rosen, a british poet which nose how to make
poetry fun for children. Their are many great poems in this book. The ones I likes best
are the following "Greedy Dog by James Hurley "Waking Up by Eleanor Farjeon, "Im
Nobody" buy Emily Dickinson and The Honey Pot by Alan Riddell. Some of Michael
Rosen's poems in the book too. I like they very much.

✔ FINAL REVIEW

Name: _____ Date: _____

Handmade Birthday Cards (164)

Would you like to make you own birth day cards. It is easy to do, and persons will
love your one-of-a kind work of art First, you will need a sheet of heavy paper. Fold
it in half. Then decorates the front panel with a design, a drawing or a photograf. You
can use markers, paint or pencils. If you use crayons press light because heavy wax
layers smear easy. After you finish the cover design, open your card, careful print a
short message, sign your name. What a great way to celebrate a family member's
special day. Oh, and don't forget to sing Happy Birthday!

✔ FINAL REVIEW

165   The Kuiper Belt

At the edge of the solar system (beyond uranus and Neptune) ~~lays~~ lies the Kuiper belt.
~~These~~ This ~~mysteryus~~ mysterious region contains many objects, some are almost as big as pluto. For
many ~~year~~ years, Pluto was called a planet. Now, many ~~scientist~~ scientists consider it ~~simple~~ simply the ~~larger~~ largest
object in the Kuiper belt. As space exploration ~~encreases~~ increases our ~~knowlege~~ knowledge of the solar
system, some old ideas are being ~~riplaced~~ replaced with more accurate ~~observashins~~ observations.

> **X**   ERRORS: MAKE UPPERCASE: 2; PERIODS: 1; SEMICOLONS: 1; COMMAS: 1;
> PARENTHESES: 1; PLURALS: 2; DEMONSTRATIVE PRONOUNS: 1;
> TRANSITIVE/INTRANSITIVE VERBS: 1; ADJECTIVES: 1; ADVERBS: 1; SPELLING: 5

166   Fauve Artists

The Fauves were a group of french artists ~~what~~ who exhibited ~~they~~ their paintings in the late
1800s and early 1900s. They were ~~enspired~~ inspired by the energy of Vincent van Gogh and
Paul Gauguin. The word *fauve* means "wild beast" in French. The name was meant to be
insulting. It wasn't chosen by the artists, it was given to the group by an art critic ~~which~~ who
did not like their work. The Fauves wanted to create ~~expressave~~ expressive work, so ~~them~~ they used
bright colors, simple shapes, and exciting brush strokes. The Fauve group ~~encluded~~ included the
following artists: Gustave Moreau, Henri Matisse, Andre Derain, and Raoul Dufy. The Fauvist
~~movemunt~~ movement did not last very long, but the artists produced some very original work.

> **X**   ERRORS: MAKE UPPERCASE: 1; SEMICOLONS: 1; COLONS: 1; COMMAS: 4;
> APOSTROPHES: 1; QUOTATION MARKS: 2; SUBJECT PRONOUNS: 1;
> POSSESSIVE PRONOUNS: 1; RELATIVE PRONOUNS: 2; SPELLING: 4

Name: _____ Date: _____

The Kuiper Belt 165

At the edge of the solar system beyond uranus and Neptune) lays the Kuiper belt. These mysteryus region contains many objects some are almost as big as pluto. For many year, Pluto was called a planet. Now, many scientist consider it simple the larger object in the Kuiper belt. As space exploration encreases our knowlege of the solar system some old ideas are being riplaced with more accurate observashins

✔ FINAL REVIEW

Name: _____ Date: _____

Fauve Artists 166

The Fauves were a group of french artists what exhibited they paintings in the late 1800s and early 1900s. They were enspired by the energy of Vincent van Gogh and Paul Gauguin. The word *fauve* means wild beast in French. The name was meant to be insulting. It wasnt chosen by the artists it was given to the group by an art critic which did not like their work. The Fauves wanted to create expressave work, so them used bright colors simple shapes and exciting brush strokes. The Fauve group encluded the following artists Gustave Moreau Henri Matisse, Andre Derain and Raoul Dufy. The Fauvist movemunt did not last very long, but the artists produced some very original work.

✔ FINAL REVIEW

167 Straddling States

Sometimes, ~~citys~~ ^{cities} grow across state or provincial ~~boundary~~ ^{boundaries}. For example, part of flin Flon (a canadian mining city) is in Saskatchewan, the other part is in manitoba. Most ~~persons~~ ^{people} in the city live on the Manitoba side. Another Canadian city, lloydminster, ~~lays~~ ^{lies} in both alberta and Saskatchewan. In the United states, the Kansas City metropolitan area (which includes the separate cities of Kansas city, Kansas and Kansas City, Missouri) straddles state boundaries. Other state-spanning urban areas include the following, Texarkana, Florala, and Lake Tahoe.

> ✗ ERRORS: MAKE UPPERCASE: 7; PERIODS: 2; SEMICOLONS: 1; COLONS: 1; HYPHENS: 1; COMMAS: 1; PARENTHESES: 2; PLURALS: 2; TRANSITIVE/INTRANSITIVE VERBS: 1; SPELLING: 1

168 Maurice Utrillo

Maurice Utrillo was a famous ~~paintir which~~ ^{painter who} was born in Paris, France. ~~He~~ ^{His} mother (Suzanne Valadon) was a painter and an artist's model. ~~Unnlike~~ ^{Unlike} the Impressionists, Utrillo (not did) work outdoors, he painted his city street scenes from memory. Sometimes, he consulted picture post cards to help ~~he~~ ^{him} remember details. Utrillo, not ^{did} follow other artists' styles, he painted in ~~her~~ ^{his} own way. His master pieces include Street in a paris Suburb with trees and L'Impasse, cottin.

> ✗ ERRORS: MAKE UPPERCASE: 3; SEMICOLONS: 2; APOSTROPHES: 2; PARENTHESES: 1; PRONOUN/NOUN AGREEMENT: 1; POSSESSIVE PRONOUNS: 1; OBJECT PRONOUNS: 1; RELATIVE PRONOUNS: 1; SPELLING: 4; INSERT MISSING WORDS: 1; TRANSPOSE WORDS: 1 PAIR

Name: _____ Date: _____

Straddling States (167)

Sometimes, citys grow across state or provincial boundary. For example, part of flin Flon (a canadian mining city is in Saskatchewan the other part is in manitoba. Most persons in the city live on the Manitoba side Another Canadian city, lloydminster, lays in both alberta and Saskatchewan. In the United states, the Kansas City metropolitan area (which includes the separate cities of Kansas city, Kansas and Kansas City, Missouri straddles state boundaries Other state spanning urban areas include the following Texarkana, Florala and Lake Tahoe.

✔ FINAL REVIEW

Name: _____ Date: _____

Maurice Utrillo (168)

Maurice Utrillo was a famous paintir which was born in Paris, France. He mother (Suzanne Valadon was a painter and an artists model. Unnlike the Impressionists, Utrillo not did work outdoors he painted his city street scenes from memory. Sometimes, he consulted picture post cards to help he remember details. Utrillo not follow other artists styles he painted in her own way. His master pieces include Street in a paris Suburb with trees and L'Impasse, cottin.

✔ FINAL REVIEW

169 | Newspaper Article

Our class was featured in the local news paper, the Sage gazette, last Sunday. A
reporter named Christine Dunn ~~finded~~ found an article about ~~we~~ us in the school newspaper,
the elementary Times, and ~~they~~ she asked to use it. The article ~~were~~ was about how we use
magazine and newspaper ~~article~~ articles to make ~~we~~ our ~~assinments~~ assignments more interesting. Every
week, ⟨visit we⟩ the school ~~libary~~ library, and our teacher challenges each of ~~them~~ us to ~~descover~~ discover
one interesting fact ~~to~~ in a magazine ~~but~~ or newspaper.

> **ERRORS:** MAKE UPPERCASE: 2; PERIODS: 1; COMMAS: 1; PLURALS: 1;
> PRONOUN/NOUN AGREEMENT: 1; POSSESSIVE PRONOUNS: 1; OBJECT PRONOUNS: 2;
> IRREGULAR PAST TENSE VERBS: 1; SUBJECT/VERB AGREEMENT: 1;
> PREPOSITIONS: 1; CONJUNCTIONS: 1; SPELLING: 4; TRANSPOSE WORDS: 1 PAIR

170 | Federico García Lorca

Federico García lorca was one of Spain's ~~most greater~~ greatest writers. He ~~writed~~ wrote many ~~poem~~ poems,
which were collected into the following three famous books, Book of Poems, Songs,
and Gypsy Ballads. He also started a dramatic company that traveled around the
country performing plays. He wrote many of ~~this~~ these plays himself. ~~Tragic,~~ Tragically García
Lorca was killed in the Spanish Civil war. Since his death, García Lorca's fame
~~have continue~~ has continued to grow. His works have been translated into english, french, German,
japanese, and many other languages.

> **ERRORS:** MAKE UPPERCASE: 5; COLONS: 1; COMMAS: 1; APOSTROPHES: 2;
> UNDERLINES: 3; PLURALS: 1; DEMONSTRATIVE PRONOUNS: 1;
> PERFECT TENSE VERBS: 1; IRREGULAR PAST TENSE VERBS: 1; ADJECTIVES: 1;
> ADVERBS: 1; DELETE EXTRA WORDS: 1

Name: _____ Date: _____

Newspaper Article ⟨169⟩

Our class was featured in the local news paper, the <u>Sage gazette</u>, last Sunday. A reporter named Christine Dunn finded an article about we in the school newspaper, the <u>elementary Times</u>, and they asked to use it The article were about how we use magazine and newspaper article to make we assinments more interesting. Every week, visit we the school libary and our teacher challenges each of them to descover one interesting fact to a magazine but newspaper.

....

Name: _____ Date: _____

Federico García Lorca ⟨170⟩

Federico García lorca was one of Spains most greater writers. He writed many poem, which were collected into the following three famous books Book of Poems, Songs, and Gypsy Ballads. He also started a dramatic company that traveled around the country performing plays. He wrote many of this plays himself. Tragic, García Lorca was killed in the Spanish Civil war. Since his death, García Lorcas fame have continue to grow. His works have been translated into english, french German, japanese, and many other languages.

171   A Multitalented Man

A great <u>b</u>ritish ~~actor~~ and ~~director~~, <u>s</u>ir John Gielgud was ~~famus~~ for his role as Hamlet in one [actor] [director] [famous]

of William Shakespeares most popular ~~tragedys~~. He played that ~~challengeing~~ part more [tragedies] [challenging]

than 500 times. Gielgud also directed many plays. Touring the world in the 1950s, he

became ~~wide~~ recognized for his solo show called <u>Ages of Man</u>. The show was composed [widely]

of well-known passages from Shakespeare's plays. Gielgud's movie career began in 1924

with the film <u>Who Is the Man?</u> His film credits include the following ~~notuble~~ pictures [notable]

<u>The Secret Agent</u>, <u>Julius Caesar</u>, <u>Becket</u>, <u>Murder on the Orient Express</u> and <u>Plenty</u>. He also

~~writed~~ the following books Early Stages, <u>An Actor and His Time</u>, and <u>Stage Directions</u>. [wrote]

> **ERRORS:** MAKE UPPERCASE: 2; COLONS: 2; HYPHENS: 1; COMMAS: 1; APOSTROPHES: 1; UNDERLINES: 3; IRREGULAR PAST TENSE VERBS: 1; ADVERBS: 1; SPELLING: 6

172   The Black Forest

The <u>b</u>lack Forest ~~be~~ a mountain range ~~to~~ southwestern Germany The range was given [is] [in]

its name by the ancient <u>r</u>omans. On the lower slopes of the mountains, oak and beech

trees ~~grows~~. At ~~highest~~ elevations, pine and fir trees crowd together ~~close~~ they ~~near~~ [grow] [higher] [closely] [nearly]

block out the sunlight. Jacob and Wilhelm Grimm ~~sets~~ many of ~~they~~ stories in the Black [set] [their]

Forest, and artists ~~has base~~ fairy-tale illustrations on ~~home~~ and villages from the region. [have based] [homes]

The following familiar Grimm tales have a forest setting: "Snow White and the Seven

Dwarfs, "Hansel and Gretel, and Little Red Riding Hood."

> **ERRORS:** MAKE UPPERCASE: 2; PERIODS: 1; SEMICOLONS: 1; QUOTATION MARKS: 3; PLURALS: 1; POSSESSIVE PRONOUNS: 1; PERFECT TENSE VERBS: 1; IRREGULAR LINKING VERBS: 1; SUBJECT/VERB AGREEMENT: 2; PREPOSITIONS: 1; ADJECTIVES: 1; ADVERBS: 2

Name: _____ Date: _____

A Multitalented Man

171

A great british acter and directer, sir John Gielgud was famus for his role as Hamlet in one of William Shakespeares most popular tragedys. He played that challengeing part more than 500 times. Gielgud also directed many plays. Touring the world in the 1950s, he became wide recognized for his solo show called <u>Ages of Man</u>. The show was composed of well known passages from Shakespeare's plays. Gielgud's movie career began in 1924 with the film <u>Who Is the Man?</u> His film credits include the following notuble pictures The Secret Agent, <u>Julius Caesar</u>, Becket, <u>Murder on the Orient Express</u> and <u>Plenty</u>. He also writed the following books <u>Early Stages</u>, An Actor and His Time, and <u>Stage Directions</u>.

✔ FINAL REVIEW

Name: _____ Date: _____

The Black Forest

172

The black Forest be a mountain range to southwestern Germany The range was given its name by the ancient romans. On the lower slopes of the mountains, oak and beech trees grows. At highest elevations, pine and fir trees crowd together close they near block out the sunlight. Jacob and Wilhelm Grimm sets many of they stories in the Black Forest, and artists has base fairy-tale illustrations on home and villages from the region. The following familiar Grimm tales have a forest setting: "Snow White and the Seven Dwarfs, "Hansel and Gretel, and Little Red Riding Hood."

✔ FINAL REVIEW

173 Autumn Afternoons

Every autumn day, the same thing happens. When Howard hears Dion calling, she stops
(he)
and turn around. Dion catches up with him, or he apologizes for being late. Howard say
(turns)   (and)   (says)
that he does not mind and he challenges Dion to a race. The two boy run to Howards
(boys)
house. The race usual ends in a tie and Howard and Dion fall down on the lawn. He
(usually)   (They)
lay there for a minute, gasping. Then, both of they go into the house. Howard makes a
(lie)   (them)
snack. They sit at the kitchen table, drink lemonade and tell jokes until 400 P.M. Dion looks
at the clock and says, Moms expecting me. Then, he hurrys home.
(hurries)

ERRORS: COLONS: 1; COMMAS: 4; APOSTROPHES: 2; QUOTATION MARKS: 2;
PLURALS: 1; PRONOUN/NOUN AGREEMENT: 2; OBJECT PRONOUNS: 1;
TRANSITIVE/INTRANSITIVE VERBS: 1; SUBJECT/VERB AGREEMENT: 2;
CONJUNCTIONS: 1; ADVERBS: 1; SPELLING: 1

174 Leif Eriksson

The viking adventurer Leif Eriksson lived in Greenland and him sailed from the Viking
(he)
settlement their. She visited the coast of North America more than 1,000 years ago. He
(there)(He)
spended the winter in a place he called vinland. Vinland had wild grapes and
(spent)
good farmland. Eriksson didnt build a settlement in Vinland. Instead he returned home
in the spring. Later, other Viking explorers builded at least one small settlement. You
(built)
can visit its ruins in Newfoundland. Historians and scientists has look for Vinland. Sum
(have looked)(Some)
believes it was in Nova scotia and others thinks it was in Newfoundland. Unfortunately,
(believe)   (think)
someone know for sure.
(no one)(knows)

ERRORS: MAKE UPPERCASE: 3; COMMAS: 3; APOSTROPHES: 1;
HOMOPHONES: 2; PRONOUN/NOUN AGREEMENT: 1; SUBJECT PRONOUNS: 1;
INDEFINITE PRONOUNS: 1; PERFECT TENSE VERBS: 1;
IRREGULAR PAST TENSE VERBS: 2; SUBJECT/VERB AGREEMENT: 3

Name: _____ Date: _____

Autumn Afternoons (173)

Every autumn day, the same thing happens. When Howard hears Dion calling she stops and turn around. Dion catches up with him, or he apologizes for being late. Howard say that he does not mind and he challenges Dion to a race. The two boy run to Howards house. The race usual ends in a tie and Howard and Dion fall down on the lawn. He lay there for a minute, gasping. Then, both of they go into the house. Howard makes a snack. They sit at the kitchen table, drink lemonade and tell jokes until 400 P.M. Dion looks at the clock and says, Moms expecting me. Then, he hurrys home.

✔ FINAL REVIEW

Name: _____ Date: _____

Leif Eriksson (174)

The viking adventurer Leif Eriksson lived in Greenland and him sailed from the Viking settlement their. She visited the coast of North America more than 1,000 years ago. He spended the winter in a place he called vinland. Vinland had wild grapes and good farmland. Eriksson didnt build a settlement in Vinland. Instead he returned home in the spring. Later, other Viking explorers builded at least one small settlement. You can visit its ruins in Newfoundland. Historians and scientists has look for Vinland. Sum believes it was in Nova scotia and others thinks it was in Newfoundland. Unfortunately, someone know for sure.

✔ FINAL REVIEW

175 Tropical Forests

There are two kinds of ~~tropicle~~ tropical forests. ~~Them~~ They are monsoon forests ~~or~~ and rain forests. Both ~~recieve~~ receive large quantities of rain fall. The ~~difference among~~ difference between the two ~~lays~~ lies in the time period when the rain falls. Monsoon forests are located in places that ~~recieve~~ receive most of ~~there~~ their moisture during a rainy season. The rest of the year is ~~relative~~ relatively dry. By contrast, rain forests grow in places where it is wet all year. In many rain forests, heavy rains fall every afternoon. In ~~none~~ some, rain seldom falls, but morning fog condenses on broad, flat leaves of the canopy and ~~drip~~ drips down to the forest floor. Monsoon forests are ~~finded~~ found in Australia, in India, and along the Brazilian coast. Rain forests thrive in the Amazon Basin, in the Congo, and in southeast Asia.

> ERRORS: MAKE UPPERCASE: 1; COMMAS: 3; HOMOPHONES: 1; SUBJECT PRONOUNS: 1; INDEFINITE PRONOUNS: 1; TRANSITIVE/INTRANSITIVE VERBS: 1; IRREGULAR PAST TENSE VERBS: 1; SUBJECT/VERB AGREEMENT: 1; PREPOSITIONS: 1; CONJUNCTIONS: 1; ADVERBS: 1; SPELLING: 6

176 Claude Debussy

Claude Debussy, a famous French composer, was born in 1862. His home childhood was located ~~to~~ in a poor neighborhood near ~~near~~ Paris, but young Claude was rich in musical talent. A very wealthy woman ~~whom~~ who heard about this hired him to play the piano. He played duets with this woman and ~~she~~ her children, and he stayed in her large, ~~beautifel~~ beautiful home when he was not in school. Debussy ~~studyed~~ studied at the Paris Conservatory, ~~what~~ which was a famous music school. Later, Debussy ~~writed~~ wrote music ~~what~~ that was ~~knew~~ new and original. His pieces, ~~who~~ which are still played today, include moonlight, The sea, and childrens Corner.

> ERRORS: MAKE UPPERCASE: 3; COMMAS: 3; APOSTROPHES: 1; HOMOPHONES: 1; POSSESSIVE PRONOUNS: 1; RELATIVE PRONOUNS: 4; IRREGULAR PAST TENSE VERBS: 1; PREPOSITIONS: 1; SPELLING: 2; DELETE EXTRA WORDS: 1; TRANSPOSE WORDS: 1 PAIR

Name: _____ Date: _____

Tropical Forests (175)

There are two kinds of tropicle forests. Them are monsoon forests or rain forests. Both recieve large quantities of rain fall. The differance among the two lays in the time period when the rain falls. Monsoon forests are located in places that recieve most of there moisture during a rainy season. The rest of the year is relative dry. By contrast rain forests grow in places where it is wet all year. In many rain forests, heavy rains fall every after noon. In none, rain seldom falls, but morning fog condenses on broad flat leaves of the canopy and drip down to the forest floor. Monsoon forests are finded in Australia in India, and along the Brazilian coast. Rain forests thrive in the Amazon Basin, in the Congo, and in southeast Asia.

FINAL REVIEW

Name: _____ Date: _____

Claude Debussy (176)

Claude Debussy, a famous French composer, was born in 1862. His home childhood was located to a poor neighborhood near near Paris but young Claude was rich in musical talent. A very wealthy woman whom heard about this hired him to play the piano. He played duets with this woman and she children and he stayed in her large, beautifell home when he was not in school. Debussy studied at the Paris Conservatory, what was a famous music school. Later, Debussy writed music what was knew and original. His pieces, who are still played today, include moonlight, The sea and childrens Corner.

FINAL REVIEW

177 Clarissa's Phone Number

To: tessa@nomail.zap
From: liza@nomail.zap

Dear Tessa,

Do you have Clarissa's number? I ~~writed~~ wrote it in my address book, ~~or~~ but my Mom ~~accidental~~ accidentally threw it away when she cleaned my room last week end. Anyway, I'm planning to call Clarissa ~~tomorow~~ tomorrow. The program's next month, and she's the chair person of ~~us~~ our group.

The boys are holding their planning meeting on Monday; the girls' meetings have been ~~rischeduled~~ rescheduled for Tuesday mornings. I want to reach every one ~~these~~ this weekend.

Your friend,
Liza

ERRORS: MAKE LOWERCASE: 1; COMMAS: 3; APOSTROPHES: 4; POSSESSIVE PRONOUNS: 1; DEMONSTRATIVE PRONOUNS: 1; IRREGULAR PAST TENSE VERBS: 1; CONJUNCTIONS: 1; ADVERBS: 1; SPELLING: 5

178 Pigeons

Pigeons belong to the same family as doves. Native to the ~~coastle~~ coastal cliffs of Europe, North africa, and South Asia, the gray bird now scrounges for crumbs in ~~city~~ cities all around the world. The first pigeons were ~~bringed~~ brought to North America in 1606. Some ~~persons~~ people consider ~~they~~ them to be pests, but pigeons ~~has help~~ have helped people. If a trained domestic pigeon (homing pigeon) is taken far from its home and ~~reeleased~~ released, it will find its way back to its roost. Pigeons have been used to carry messages when other kinds of ~~communicashun~~ communication were ~~empractical~~ impractical. Many ~~country~~ countries have awarded medals to pigeons that carried important information in times of war. There is even a group of pigeon enthusiasts called the national pigeon association.

ERRORS: MAKE UPPERCASE: 4; COMMAS: 2; PARENTHESES: 1; PLURALS: 3; OBJECT PRONOUNS: 1; PERFECT TENSE VERBS: 1; IRREGULAR PAST TENSE VERBS: 1; SPELLING: 4

Name: _____ Date: _____

Clarissa's Phone Number (177)

To: tessa@nomail.zap
From: liza@nomail.zap

Dear Tessa

Do you have Clarissas number? I writed it in my address book, or my Mom accidental threw it away when she cleaned my room last week end. Anyway I'm planning to call Clarissa tomorow. The programs next month, and shes the chair person of us group. The boys are holding their planning meeting on Monday; the girls meetings have been rischeduled for Tuesday mornings. I want to reach every one these weekend.

Your friend
Liza

✔ FINAL REVIEW

Name: _____ Date: _____

Pigeons (178)

Pigeons belong to the same family as doves. Native to the coastle cliffs of Europe North africa and South Asia, the gray bird now scrounges for crumbs in city all around the world. The first pigeons were bringed to North America in 1606. Some persons consider they to be pests, but pigeons has help people. If a trained domestic pigeon (homing pigeon is taken far from its home and reeleased, it will find its way back to its roost. Pigeons have been used to carry messages when other kinds of communicashun were empractical. Many country have awarded medals to pigeons that carried important information in times of war. There is even a group of pigeon enthusiasts called the national pigeon association.

✔ FINAL REVIEW

179 An Inspiring Guest Speaker

Yesterday, every one gathered in the auditorium. "I am delighted to introduce our guest speaker, Jacob Hendrik" the principle said. I hope you enjoy he presentation."

Mr. Hendrik was a dutch college student who rided his bicicle across canada. He did it to rise money for childs in Africa. He gathered pledges from as many people as possible among the way. He kept a journle every day. Jacob used he notes to write several articles about his adventures. He saw many interesting sights on his trip. He had sum trouble on his journey too. He had to fix his bike several time once, he had to order a new set of petals.

We all enjoyed his talk. Following his example, I writed in my journal last night.

ERRORS: MAKE UPPERCASE: 2; SEMICOLONS: 1; COMMAS: 1; QUOTATION MARKS: 1; PLURALS: 2; HOMOPHONES: 3; POSSESSIVE PRONOUNS: 2; TRANSITIVE/INTRANSITIVE VERBS: 1; IRREGULAR PAST TENSE VERBS: 2; PREPOSITIONS: 1; SPELLING: 3

180 The Reporter's Visit

Sometimes, our local news paper prints articles about schools. A reporter, David Casey, visited to our class today. He was delihted to here about our class project. He thinks it will make an unnusual story. We have been keeping journals since the beginning of the year. At first, we had troubal thinking of things to write about but our teacher teached we how to find interesting ideas in every day events. We have written about every subject. Some students include skeches in their journals. Im not able to draw well, so I dont add pictures. My friend Jacks entrys always make me laugh. The reporter enterviewed several of us and him may include selections from our journals his article.

ERRORS: COMMAS: 2; APOSTROPHES: 3; HOMOPHONES: 1; SUBJECT PRONOUNS: 1; OBJECT PRONOUNS: 1; IRREGULAR PAST TENSE VERBS: 1; SPELLING: 8; DELETE EXTRA WORDS: 1; INSERT MISSING WORDS: 1

Name: _____ Date: _____

An Inspiring Guest Speaker (179)

Yesterday, every one gathered in the auditorium. "I am delighted to introduce our guest speaker, Jacob Hendrik" the principle said. I hope you enjoy he presentation."

Mr. Hendrik was a dutch college student who rided his bicicle across canada. He did it to rise money for childs in Africa. He gathered pledges from as many people as possible among the way. He kept a journle every day. Jacob used he notes to write several articles about his adventures. He saw many interesting sights on his trip. He had sum trouble on his journey too. He had to fix his bike several time once, he had to order a new set of petals. We all enjoyed his talk. Following his example, I writed in my journal last night.

Name: _____ Date: _____

The Reporter's Visit (180)

Sometimes, our local news paper prints articles about schools. A reporter, David Casey, visited to our class today. He was delihted to here about our class project. He thinks it will make an unnusual story. We have been keeping journals since the beginning of the year. At first, we had troubal thinking of things to write about but our teacher teached we how to find interesting ideas in every day events. We have written about every subject. Some students include skeches in their journals. Im not able to draw well, so I dont add pictures. My friend Jacks entrys always make me laugh. The reporter enterviewed several of us and him may include selections from our journals his article.

End of Book Test: Swans and Ducks

Swans are large, beautiful birds. ~~None~~ Some are white, some are black, and some are both black and white. They're ~~finded~~ found in many parts of the world. When most people think of a swan, ~~them~~ they imagine a graceful creature gliding across a lake in a city garden. This type of bird is called a mute swan. It isn't native to North america, its distant relatives were ~~bringed~~ brought to Europe from Asia. Although the word *mute* means "silent," mute swans ~~is~~ are not always quiet, they can hiss, grunt, or even bark. A baby swan is called a cygnet. A cygnet's Mother is called a pen, and its father is called a cob. Male swans are ~~usual~~ usually one-third ~~largest~~ larger than females.

Have you ever seen ducks swimming in a lake or pond? Chances are, ~~this~~ those were mallards. Mallards are common in North America, Europe, and Asia. The mallard is called a dabbling duck because ~~they~~ it finds its food close ~~two~~ to the surface of the water instead of diving deep into a lake. Items on a mallard's menu include the following: snails, insects, tadpoles, frogs, small fish, ~~but~~ and fish eggs. ~~Unfortunate~~ Unfortunately for mallards, they are on the menus of many mammals, including ~~fox~~ foxes, coyotes, and bob cats. They defend ~~themselfs~~ themselves by flying, swimming, or staying very still. If they remain ~~motionluss~~ motionless, they blend into the shadows of ~~they~~ their favorite (places hiding). Female ducks (hens) ~~lie~~ lay eggs every spring.

In ~~the~~ "The Ugly Duckling," an outcast duckling turns out to be a cygnet and turns ~~onto~~ into a beautiful swan. Everyone—even the ducklings that ~~has make~~ have made fun of ~~he~~ him—thought he was beautiful. The moral of the story ~~be~~ is that inner beauty always wins over outer beauty.

For more fascinating facts ~~facts~~ about swans and ducks, read Waterfowl by Steven Madge and Hilary burn. What a great book!

> ERRORS: MAKE UPPERCASE: 2; MAKE LOWERCASE: 1; PERIODS: 1; SEMICOLONS: 2; COLONS: 1; HYPHENS: 1; COMMAS: 3; APOSTROPHES: 2; QUOTATION MARKS: 2; QUESTION MARKS: 1; EXCLAMATION POINTS: 1; UNDERLINES: 1; PARENTHESES: 1; DASHES: 1; PLURALS: 2; HOMOPHONES: 1; PRONOUN/NOUN AGREEMENT: 1; SUBJECT PRONOUNS: 1; POSSESSIVE PRONOUNS: 1; OBJECT PRONOUNS: 1; DEMONSTRATIVE PRONOUNS: 1; INDEFINITE PRONOUNS: 1; RELATIVE PRONOUNS: 1; TRANSITIVE/INTRANSITIVE VERBS: 1; PERFECT TENSE VERBS: 1; IRREGULAR PAST TENSE VERBS: 2; IRREGULAR LINKING VERBS: 1; SUBJECT/VERB AGREEMENT: 1; PREPOSITIONS: 1; CONJUNCTIONS: 1; ADJECTIVES: 1; ADVERBS: 2; SPELLING: 2; DELETE EXTRA WORDS: 1; INSERT MISSING WORDS: 1; TRANSPOSE WORDS: 1 PAIR

Name: _____   Date: _____

End of Book Test: Swans and Ducks

Swans are large beautiful birds. None are white, some are black, and some are both black and white. Theyre finded in many parts of the world. When most people think of a swan, them imagine a graceful creature gliding across a lake in a city garden. This type of bird is called a mute swan. It isn't native to North america its distant relatives were bringed to Europe from Asia. Although the word *mute* means silent," mute swans is not always quiet they can hiss, grunt or even bark. A baby swan is called a cygnet. A cygnet's Mother is called a pen, and its father is called a cob. Male swans are usual one third largest than females.

Have you ever seen ducks swimming in a lake or pond. Chances are, this were mallards Mallards are common in North America, Europe, and Asia. The mallard is called a dabbling duck because they finds its food close two the surface the water instead of diving deep into a lake. Items on a mallards menu include the following snails insects, tadpoles, frogs, small fish, but fish eggs. Unfortunate for mallards, they are on the menus of many mammals, including fox, coyotes, and bob cats. They defend themselfs by flying, swimming, or staying very still. If they remain motionluss, they blend into the shadows of they favorite places hiding. Female ducks (hens lie eggs every spring.

In the "The Ugly Duckling, an outcast duckling turns out to be a cygnet and turns onto a beautiful swan. Everyone—even the ducklings that has make fun of he thought he was beautiful. The moral of the story be that inner beauty always wins over outer beauty.

For more fascinating facts facts about swans and ducks, read Waterfowl by Steven Madge and Hilary burn. What a great book.

Proofreader's Marks Chart

MARK	MEANING	EXAMPLE
≡	**Use an uppercase letter.**	Kathy lives in canada.
/	**Use a lowercase letter.**	My mom is my uncle's Sister.
⊙	**Insert a period.**	This is my book⊙
^;	**Insert a semicolon.**	It was a hot day^ the temperature was 100°F.
^:	**Insert a colon.**	The game will start at 2^00 P.M.
? ^	**Insert a question mark.**	Is this your book^
! ^	**Insert an exclamation point.**	What a great book^
^,	**Insert a comma.**	I will visit you on July 20^ 2012.
’ V	**Insert an apostrophe.**	Don’t lose your backpack.
“ V ” V	**Insert quotation marks.**	I will come to your party, said Blake.
- ^	**Insert a hyphen.**	I finished two^thirds of my work.
___	**Underline a title.**	Her favorite movie is The Wizard of Oz.
( )	**Insert parentheses.**	Arachnids (spiders) have eight legs.
— ^	**Insert a dash.**	Nothing scared him^not even snakes.
___	**Correct the spelling or word choice error.**	I love my dog ~~becuz~~ because she is playful.
⁀ ‿	**Close space between words.**	I finished my home work quickly.
___ᘓ	**Delete.**	I do not want ice ~~ice~~ cream.
^	**Insert a word or phrase.**	Mr. Lane is^ my teacher.
∽	**Transpose letters or words.**	Today is the day first of school.

Editing Checklist

☐ Each sentence begins with an uppercase letter.

☐ Proper nouns and titles begin with uppercase letters.

☐ Each sentence ends with a period, a question mark, or an exclamation point.

☐ Commas, colons, semicolons, parentheses, and dashes are used in the correct places.

☐ Possessive nouns and contractions have apostrophes.

☐ Quotation marks are used around dialogue; story, song, and poem titles; and definitions.

☐ Book and movie titles are underlined.

☐ Hyphens are used in fractions and in appropriate compound nouns or modifiers.

☐ Each verb is correctly used and agrees with its subject.

☐ Each pronoun is correctly used and agrees with the noun it represents.

☐ Prepositions, conjunctions, adjectives, and adverbs are used correctly.

☐ Each sentence is clear and complete.

☐ All words are spelled correctly.

Grammar Glossary

adjective: a word that describes a person, place, or thing. For example, the words *tall, blue, old, scared,* and *big* are adjectives. (See **comparative adjective** and **superlative adjective**.)

adverb: a word that modifies a verb or an adjective. Many adverbs end with the suffix *ly*. For example, *An **extremely** tall boy walked **slowly** across the playground.*

apostrophe: a punctuation mark (') used to show that someone owns or possesses something. For example, *Alice's apron was white.* (See **possessive**.) It is also used to show missing letters in contractions. For example, the word *cannot* becomes *can't*.

capitalization: An uppercase letter is used at the beginning of each of the following words:

- the first word in a sentence or quotation

- the name of a person or an animal, such as a pet

- the name of a city, country, sports team, or planet

- the important words in the title of a book, story, film, poem, work of art, business, or organization

- abbreviations of personal and official titles, such as *Mr., Ms., Dr.,* and *Gov.*

colon: a punctuation mark (:) used to introduce a formal list. For example, *The following boys will be on the team: Mark, George, Tom, and Sam.* Colons are also used to separate hours from minutes. For example, *8:25 P.M.*

comma: a punctuation mark (,) that marks a separation within a sentence. It is used in the following ways:

- after the number of the day and before the year in a date

- between the city and state or country in a place name

- after the greeting and closing in a letter

- between items in a series or consecutive adjectives

- before a conjunction at the beginning of an independent sentence clause

- after introductory words or phrases and before and after some parenthetical words or phrases

comparative adjective: an adjective that compares two things. For example, *This box is **bigger** than that one.*

contraction: a combination of two words. In a contraction, an apostrophe stands for missing letters. For example, in the contraction *don't,* the apostrophe stands for the missing *o* in *not*. Contractions are used in conversation and informal writing.

coordinating conjunction: a conjunction that joins two independent clauses within the same sentence. The word that precedes the coordinating conjunction is always followed by a comma. For example, *Johann went to the store, **and** he bought some milk.*

Grammar Glossary

dash: a punctuation mark (—) used to show sudden breaks or interruptions in a sentence. For example, *Mike—my best friend in the whole world—is coming over to play video games.*

exclamation point: a punctuation mark (!) used to show strong feelings. For example, *Wow! What a terrific football card!*

homophone: one of two or more words that sound the same but are spelled differently and have different meanings. For example, *The **two** of us will come **to** the park **too**.*

hyphen: a punctuation mark (-) used to join fraction words and compound nouns and modifiers. For example, *One-half of my family went to my great-grandfather's birthday party.*

parentheses: a set of punctuation marks ( ) used to set apart definitions or other extra information within a sentence. For example, *The Tyrannosaurus rex was a carnivore (meat eater).*

period: a punctuation mark (.) used at the end of a sentence that is not a question or an exclamation. Periods are also used after most abbreviations.

plural: a form of a noun that means more than one

- Most regular plurals are formed by adding an *s* (*two **boys***).

- Plurals of words that end with *x* or *s* are usually formed by adding *es* (*two **boxes***).

- One type of irregular plural is the same as the singular form. These special words include *deer, moose,* and *trout.*

(**plural** continued)
- Other irregular plurals are different and must be memorized. These irregular plurals include some very common words, such as *men, women, children,* and *people.*

possessive: a word form that shows ownership

- Singular possessive nouns are created by adding *'s*. For example, ***Anna's** dog is cute.*

- Most plural possessive nouns are created by adding an apostrophe. For example, *The **boys'** team won the spelling bee.*

- Irregular plural possessives add *'s*. For example, *The **children's** concert is on Friday.*

prefix: letters added to the beginning of a word to modify the meaning of the word. For example, ***re**grow, **dis**agree, **un**realistic, **bi**cycle, **im**possible,* and ***mis**understand.*

preposition: a word that links a noun or pronoun to other words in the same sentence. Prepositions show relationships between words or phrases. For example, *The friends played **in** the backyard.*

pronoun: a word that takes the place of a noun. The words *he, she, it, we,* and *they* are pronouns. The pronoun *I* is always capitalized. Pronouns must agree with the nouns they replace. For example, ***Mike** went to the store. **He** bought a game.*

proper noun: a noun that names a specific thing, such as a person, a city, a country, a street, a school, a holiday, or a historical event. Proper nouns are always capitalized. (See **capitalization**.)

Grammar Glossary

question mark: a punctuation mark (?) used at the end of a question

quotation mark: A set of these punctuation marks (" ") is used around dialogue, or words that someone says. One mark comes before the first word the person says, and the other mark comes after the last word the person says. For example, *"Did you do the homework?" Jason asked.*

semicolon: a punctuation mark (;) that can be used instead of a coordinating conjunction to join two independent clauses. For example, *I spotted her; I waved.*

subject: a noun phrase that tells what a sentence is about. For example, **The boy** *runs home.*

suffix: letters added to the end of a word to modify the meaning of the word. For example, *quick**ly**, care**ful**, enjoy**ment**, writ**er**,* and *sugges**tion**.*

superlative adjective: an adjective that compares three or more things. For example, *This is the **biggest** box of all.*

tense: a form of a verb that shows when the action takes place. (See **verb**.) Verbs can be in past, present, or future tense. Each of these tenses also has a perfect tense. Present tense verbs have two forms. One form is used with singular nouns. The other form is used with plural nouns. For example, *He **walks**,* but *They **walk**.* Most verbs form the past tense by adding *ed.* Some verbs have irregular past tense forms. Some common irregular past tense forms include *had, gave, did,* and *ran.* Most future tense verbs are formed by adding *will* before a present tense action verb. The verb appears in a different form than in the present tense. For example, *She **eats**,* but *She **will eat**.* Most perfect tense verbs are formed by adding *have* before a specific tense of a verb. For example, *We **had eaten** dinner, We **have eaten** dinner,* and *We **will have eaten** dinner.*

verb: a word that shows an action. Verbs have past, present, and future forms called *tenses.* (See **tense**.) Each verb in a sentence must agree with its subject. (See **subject**.)

word root: letters that form the root or base of a word without prefixes of suffixes. Word roots often come from Greek or Latin words or word parts. For example, *bio**graph**y, **geo**logy, bi**cycle**.*